# *MORE* GRAMMAR GAMES

### Cognitive, affective and movement activities for EFL students

## MARIO RINVOLUCRI AND PAUL DAVIS

### CAMBRIDGE
UNIVERSITY PRESS

Published by the Press Syndicate of the University of Cambridge
The Pitt Building, Trumpington Street, Cambridge CB2 1RP
40 West 20th Street, New York, NY 10011-4211, USA
10 Stamford Road, Oakleigh, Melbourne 3166, Australia

© Cambridge University Press 1995

First published 1995

Printed in Great Britain
by Scotprint Ltd, Musselburgh, Scotland

Library of Congress cataloguing in publication data applied for

A catalogue record for this book is available from the British Library

ISBN 0 521 46630 X

# Contents

CONTENTS

# Map of the book

| | GAME | GRAMMAR | LEVEL | TIME |
|---|---|---|---|---|
| 1.1 | Betting on grammar horses | * Verbs + -ing / verbs + infinitive / verbs that take either | * Upper intermediate | 30 – 45 minutes |
| 1.2 | Happy grammar families | * Basic word order | * Beginner | 30 – 40 minutes |
| 1.3 | Grammar Reversi | * Phrasal verbs | * Upper intermediate | 50 minutes |
| 1.4 | Three from six grammar quiz | Varied | Elementary to advanced | 15 – 25 minutes |
| 1.5 | Present perfect love story | Present perfect simple, continuous, active and passive | Lower intermediate and intermediate | 40 – 60 minutes |
| 1.6 | Spoof | * (1) Present continuous (2) Adjective / noun collocation | * (1) Intermediate * (2) Advanced | 30 minutes |
| 1.7 | Student created text | * Continuous tenses | * Intermediate to upper intermediate | 60 minutes |
| 1.8 | Speed | * Collocations with wide, narrow and broad | * Intermediate to advanced | 15 – 20 minutes |
| 1.9 | I challenge | Word endings and suffixes | Beginner to advanced | 25 minutes |
| 1.10 | The triangle game | Prepositions Adverbs of time, place and movement | Intermediate and above | 40 – 50 minutes |
| 2.1 | One becomes two | Varied syntax and grammar | Elementary to advanced | 20 – 30 minutes |
| 2.2 | Mind-reading | Varied | Beginner to intermediate | 20 – 30 minutes |
| 2.3 | Weed-read | * Varied | * (1) Lower intermediate * (2) Advanced | 15 – 25 minutes |
| 2.4 | Don't 'she' me | Word-building | Intermediate to advanced | 45 minutes |
| 2.5 | Final word | Word position | * Intermediate | 30 – 40 minutes |
| 2.6 | DIY word order | Word order | Beginner to advanced | 15 – 25 minutes |
| 2.7 | Body tense map | Tenses and their uses | Elementary to advanced | 30 – 45 minutes |
| 2.8 | Shunting words | Syntax, especially clause coordination | Elementary to advanced | 20 – 40 minutes |
| 2.9 | Mending sentences | Varied | Post beginner to advanced | 20 – 30 minutes |
| 2.10 | Hinged sentences | Syntax and punctuation | * Intermediate | 20 – 30 minutes |
| 2.11 | Spot the differences | * Common mistakes | * Elementary | 20 – 30 minutes |
| 2.12 | Self-generated language | Varied | Post beginner to elementary | 30 – 50 minutes |

* This activity can be adapted for use with other grammatical structures.

* This activity can be adapted to suit different levels.

| | GAME | GRAMMAR | LEVEL | TIME |
|---|---|---|---|---|
| **3.1** | Achievements | * *By* + time phrases<br>Past perfect | Lower intermediate | 20 – 30 minutes |
| **3.2** | Typical questions | Question formation – varied interrogatives | Beginner to elementary | 20 – 30 minutes |
| **3.3** | Did you write that? | Verbs of liking and disliking + gerund<br>Past question form with relative pronoun<br>Reported speech | Elementary to intermediate | 30 – 45 minutes |
| **3.4** | Who wrote what about me? | * Verbs that take the gerund | * Lower to upper intermediate | 30 – 40 minutes |
| **3.5** | In-groups and out-groups | * Varied interrogatives | * Elementary to advanced | 20 – 40 minutes |
| **3.6** | Verbs for extroverts | Verbs followed by *with* (reciprocal verbs) | Intermediate to advanced | 20 – 30 minutes |
| **3.7** | *To* versus *-ing* | Verbs + *-ing* / verbs + infinitive with *to* | Upper intermediate to advanced | 3 minutes in first class<br>20 – 30 minutes in second class |
| **3.8** | Telling people what they feel | Imperative, imperative with *don't*, *stop* + gerund, *mind you …*, *never mind about -ing* | Intermediate to advanced | 40 – 50 minutes |
| **3.9** | Reported advice | Modals and modals reported | Elementary to intermediate | 15 – 20 minutes |
| **3.10** | Impersonating members of a set | Present and past simple – active and passive | Elementary to intermediate | 20 – 30 minutes |
| **3.11** | Choosing the passive | Past simple passive *versus* past simple active | Intermediate | 40 – 50 minutes |
| **3.12** | A sprinkling of people | Collective nouns | Upper intermediate to advanced | 50 – 60 minutes |
| **3.13** | Us lot | Quantifiers | Elementary to intermediate | 20 – 30 minutes |
| **3.14** | Lack | Noun to adjective transformation adding *less* | Upper intermediate to advanced | 40 – 50 minutes |
| **3.15** | Haves and have-nots | Multiple uses of the verb *have* | Intermediate to advanced | 40 – 50 minutes |
| **3.16** | Picture the past | Past simple, past perfect, future in the past | Lower intermediate | 20 – 40 minutes |
| **3.17** | Passive verbs | Transitive verbs usually found in the passive | Advanced | Homework and 30 – 40 minutes in class |
| **4.1** | Whose am I? | *'s* genitive + animate + human | Beginner | 15 – 20 minutes |
| **4.2** | No backshift | Reported speech without backshift after past reporting verbs | Elementary to lower intermediate | 15 – 20 minutes |
| **4.3** | Incomparable | Comparative structures | Elementary | 15 – 20 minutes |

* This activity can be adapted for use with other grammatical structures.

* This activity can be adapted to suit different levels.

MAP OF THE BOOK

| | GAME | GRAMMAR | LEVEL | TIME |
|---|---|---|---|---|
| 4.4 | Round the circle | Prepositions of movement | Beginner to elementary | 10 – 20 minutes |
| 4.5 | Eyes shut | * Present perfect | * Elementary to intermediate | 15 – 25 minutes |
| 4.6 | One question behind | Assorted interrogative forms | Beginner to intermediate | 5 – 10 minutes |
| 4.7 | Intensive talk | Present tenses and language of description | Post beginner to advanced | 40 – 50 minutes |
| 4.8 | Two against the group | Past interrogatives | Lower intermediate to advanced | 3 minutes in first class 15 – 30 minutes in second class |
| 5.1 | Real time | Language for telling the time | Beginner to post beginner | 20 – 40 minutes |
| 5.2 | Sit down then | *Who* + simple past interrogative Telling the time | Beginner to elementary | 10 – 20 minutes |
| 5.3 | Do you like your neighbours' words? | Present simple questions + short answers *Ones* (substitute word) Possessive pronouns | Post beginner | 45 minutes |
| 5.4 | Turn round quick | Irregular verbs | Elementary | 20 – 30 minutes |
| 5.5 | Only if ... | Polite requests *-ing* participle *Only if* + target language | Elementary + | 15 – 20 minutes |
| 5.6 | Future chairs | * Future forms | * Lower intermediate | 30 minutes |
| 5.7 | *If* + present perfect | * *If* + present perfect *I'd like you to* + infinitive Past interrogative | Elementary to intermediate | 15 – 20 minutes |
| 5.8 | If you had the chance | * 'Second' conditional | * Intermediate | 25 minutes |
| 5.9 | Moving Ludo (Pachisi) | Varied | * Intermediate | 60 minutes |
| 6.1 | Iffy sentences | Varied | Upper intermediate to advanced | 30 – 40 minutes |
| 6.2 | Two-faced sentences | Varied – special emphasis on syntax | Upper intermediate to very advanced | 30 – 45 minutes |
| 6.3 | Grammar homophones | Revision of irregular verbs | Intermediate to advanced | 20 minutes homework and 20 – 30 minutes in class |
| 6.4 | Written conversations | Varied | Elementary to advanced | 30 – 40 minutes |
| 6.5 | The world of take | Some basic meanings of the verb *take*, in particle verbs | Intermediate to advanced | 40 – 50 minutes |
| 6.6 | Coherence poems | Juxtaposition and coherence as the main syntactic feature | Elementary to advanced | 30 – 40 minutes |
| 6.7 | Two-word verbs | Compound verbs | Upper intermediate to advanced | 40 – 50 minutes |

* This activity can be adapted for use with other grammatical structures.

* This activity can be adapted to suit different levels.

MAP OF THE BOOK

| | GAME | GRAMMAR | LEVEL | TIME |
|---|---|---|---|---|
| **7.1** | The woman on the roof | Present continuous | Elementary | 30 – 40 minutes |
| **7.2** | Umbrella | Modals and present simple | Elementary to intermediate | 30 – 40 minutes |
| **7.3** | Eyes | 'Second' conditional | Lower to upper intermediate | 30 – 45 minutes |
| **7.4** | A dictionary game | Comparatives, *it* (referring back) | Elementary | 45 minutes |
| **7.5** | Near future seen from distant future | Past perfect and past simple | Intermediate to advanced | 30 – 40 minutes |
| **8.1** | Just a minute | Varied | Elementary to very advanced | 20 – 30 minutes |
| **8.2** | Correction letters | What the student needs to have corrected | Elementary to advanced | 15 minutes preparation time per student |
| **8.3** | Reformulation | What comes up – most relevant with students who share the same mother tongue | Beginner to advanced | 20 minutes preparation time 15 – 30 minutes in class |
| **8.4** | Mistakes mirror | Varied – for use with students who share the same mother tongue | Beginner to elementary | 15 – 20 minutes |
| **8.5** | Hand on hand | Present simple third person singular | Beginner to elementary | 15 minutes |
| **9.1** | Listening to time | * Time phrases | Upper intermediate to very advanced | 40 – 50 minutes |
| **9.2** | Guess the sentence | Varied | Beginner to intermediate | 20 minutes |
| **9.3** | Grammar letters | * 'Second' conditional | * Lower intermediate | 15 minutes preparation 10 minutes in first class |
| **9.4** | 'The' and 'a' | Articles / *another* / *the other* / *the last* / *one* / *ones* | Beginner | 25 minutes |
| **9.5** | Word order dictation | * Word order at sentence level Reflexive phrases | Intermediate | 20 – 30 minutes |
| **9.6** | Guess my grammar | Varied + question forms | Elementary to intermediate | 55 minutes |
| **9.7** | Teacherless task | Past simple and past perfect | (1) Upper intermediate to advanced (2) Intermediate | 15 – 30 minutes |
| **9.8** | Puzzle stories | Simple present and simple past interrogative forms | Beginner | 30 minutes |

* This activity can be adapted for use with other grammatical structures.

* This activity can be adapted to suit different levels.

MAP OF THE BOOK

# Introduction

Most learners somehow accept that the sounds of a foreign language are going to be different from those of their mother tongue. What is much more difficult to accept is that the grammar of the new language is also spectacularly different from the way the mother tongue works. For example, a speaker of a Latin-based language **has** 23 years, (*elle a 23 ans*), she **has** cold, she **has** hunger etc. At a subconscious, semiconscious and conscious level it is very hard to want to switch to: I **am** twenty three, I **am** cold, I **am** hungry. If it is *avere* (to have) in Italian, why should it suddenly be *essere* (to be) in English? To the Latin speaker there is something outlandish about the verb *to be* in these contexts.

There are many subconsciously contentious areas when a person begins to try to speak a foreign language. Take the interrogative and negative in English – how come these can be signalled by an intrusive extra verb: **make** you like white coffee? she **makes** not live here, what **made** you do yesterday evening? (By substituting **make** for **do** I hope I have given you an idea of how ludicrously out-of-place and meaning-blocking the auxiliaries *do*, *does*, and *did* can sound, feel and look to a person trying to use English for the first time!)

Teaching the grammar of English is not simply a question of handing out clear, linguistic information to the learners. If this were the case, teaching language would be an easier job. Somehow you, the teacher, have to induce, seduce and persuade your student into really accepting and mentally creating weird and wonderful sentences like: **do** you like white coffee?

This book provides you with practical ways of inducing your students to preconsciously feel, think and finally produce the grammar that is specific to English.

## Who can you use this book with?

Many of the exercises in this book are adaptable to any teaching situation with different grammar components, but the following starting points might be useful for you:

If you teach **primary school children**, you might start by going for the 'Movement and grammar' and 'Competitive games' sections of the book.

If you teach **adult evening classes** to which people come tired from work, you may well find things in 'Movement and grammar' that will wake them up. Do you need fresh ways of leading these whacked-out students into unknown grammar areas? If so, the 'Presentation' section will help you.

If you teach **lower secondary pupils**, you probably need a variety of ways of correcting their language. Increase your range by looking at Section 8 'Correction'. A second obvious section for you is 'Competitive games' as these activities suit the age group. If you are teaching the more academically inclined children, then have a look at 'Cognitive games'.

If you teach **upper secondary** and **tertiary** students, then 'Feelings and grammar', 'Cognitive games' and 'Meaning and translation' could be the most rewarding sections for you to look at first.

Some EFL teachers reckon that joyous ludic exercises, like the ones we have brought together here, have no place in teaching **Business English**. Our experience suggests that this view has more to do with teacher fears than student disposition. If you present game activities within a goal-orientated frame, then fully fledged business people instantly see the point. They are a prime target for this book.

If you work with **initial EFL teacher trainees**, you will find this book is a useful quarry of easily understandable and productive lesson plans for them to try out with their teaching practice classes. It is also a good resource book for them to take with them to their first teaching job. It is richer and broader than its elder sister, *Grammar games*.

If you train **in-service teachers**, you will find that certain exercises in the book are excellent discussion starters, leading into areas of theory you want to put on the trainees' map. For example, the 'Listening to people' section could well lead into discussion of the listening state of mind a skillful teacher needs.

## What's in this book?

This is a chapter-by-chapter guide to what's in the book. There is also information at the top of each activity about the grammar, level, time and materials needed. As we've already mentioned above, many activities can be adapted to different classes with different grammar components. When this is possible, it is indicated in a box at the top of the activity.

### Section 1  Competitive games

Here you will find traditional games like Happy Families and Reversi (Othello) used to sharpen the students' knowledge of areas of grammar. This section also uses formats taken from radio and TV games. It makes sense to borrow happy contexts from the students' world of entertainment.

Competitive activities that pit pairs against pairs and threes against threes are excellent for fostering collaboration and mutual help within each team. In this heightened atmosphere a lot of learning takes place without the students noticing they are 'studying'.

In many of these activities the students' language task is to look at a set of sentences and decide which are correct and which are wrong. We believe that this testing of their own criteria is central to students building up a strong internal monitor to help them speak and write correctly. We do not go along with the behaviourist hypothesis that a student who sees a wrong sentence will imprint it and retain it as correct.

This section mostly offers you activity frames that you can reuse many times, slotting in the grammar *you* want your students to work on, rather than the area we have presented in the unit. So you may want to use a game to which we have given, say, an elementary grammar content at upper intermediate level.

## Section 2  Cognitive games (Silent Way)

This section is a direct development from Section II in *Grammar Games*, 'Collaborative sentence-making games'. If you take the two sections together you have an unparalleled range of thought-provoking sentence manipulations. They are 'thought-provoking' because these exercises are mostly open-ended ones, unlike the sentence transformation exercises you find in many grammar workbooks and tests, where there is only intended to be one right answer. How do 'open-ended' transformations work? Let's take an example: in 'One becomes two' (2.1) you ask the students to expand one sentence into two utterances by adding either one or two words. So, from a single sentence like: 'do please come round and see us', students produce pairs of utterances like these: (the student additions are given in bold)

 1  Do please come round **tonight**. **Come** and see us.
 2  Do **not go**. Please come round and see us.
 3  Do **you understand**? Please come round and see us.
 4  **Yes**, I do. Please come round and see us.
 5  Do please come round and see us. **May we?**
 6  Do **your best**. Please come round and see us.
 7  Do please **feel free**. Come round and see us.
 8  **You** do **understand**? Please come round and see us.
 9  Do please come. **Drop** round and see us.
10  Do please come round and see **them**. **Not** us.

As you can see, the above exercise is not only open-ended but also multi-level. An elementary student is likely to be able to produce pairs 2 and 3, while 9 requires a good feel for colloquial English. The exercises in this section are ideal for mixed-level classes, precisely because they are open-ended. And though the exercises are mostly open-ended, you can confidently predict that the students will focus on certain areas of grammar. Six of the ten double utterances above explore various uses of *do*. If we ask students to expand the sentence: 'I am a hotel', by adding one word or two to the original four, we can predict certain structures coming up from some of the people in a lower intermediate group:

> present continuous: I am **managing** a hotel.
> negative: I am **not buying** a hotel. / I am **not** a hotel.
> passive: I am **called** a hotel.
> reporting: "I am a hotel" **he added**.
> adjective order: I am a **marvellous** hotel **porter**.
> etc.

When doing these open-ended, creative, sentence manipulation exercises with a class you will find out a lot about their grammar thinking. They may learn as much from wrong transformations as they do from being right first time. For example, is 'I am a hotel' *wrong*, or could it be said by a parent about their children or in the context of a wrong telephone number?

All this kind of work is based on Caleb Gattegno's 'Silent Way' approach in which the students discover the regularities of the language by tightly teacher-guided trial and error work. Gattegno gives the students a narrow frame and then complete creative freedom within the frame. It is amazing what students can discover for themselves if the teacher genuinely and attentively stands back and lets them get on with it. Though the discovery work done by the student is fiercely cognitive, it is clear that the unconscious resources of the mind are also fully harnessed because, from our observations, student retention of new material is remarkable.

## Section 3  Feelings and grammar

While the Competitive and Cognitive games sections focus the students' attention on the grammar, in this section the students concentrate on expressing real things about themselves and people round them. They do this using prescribed structures. They absorb the grammar, as it were, through peripheral vision. With some types of learner this is much more effective than direct, primary focus on the grammar.

In 'Choosing the passive' (3.11) students think of their early childhood and decide which of these parallel sentences best describes their situation:

| | |
|---|---|
| I was born. | I came out of my mother's womb. |
| I was taught to yawn. | I gave my first yawn. |
| I was loved by my Mum. | I loved my Mum. |

A semantically focussed exercise like this makes clear that the choice between active and passive is a motivated one.

This section draws quite strongly on areas of grammar pin-pointed by the *Collins COBUILD English Grammar*, edited by John Sinclair. So, for example, 'Verbs for extroverts', (3.6) deals with what *COBUILD* classifies as 'reciprocal verbs', e.g. *to mix with, to clash with, to compete with, to quarrel with, to consult with* etc. The *Collins COBUILD English Grammar* is rich in very useful lists of words that behave in regular grammatical ways, drawn from the huge *COBUILD* data base, but these lists have to be brought to life for students. This is what we have done in some units in this section.

'Feelings and grammar' is a further exploration of the area opened up by Gertrude Moskowitz in *Caring and Sharing in the Foreign Language Classroom*, and then continued in *Grammar in Action Again*, by Christine Frank and Mario Rinvolucri.

## Section 4  Listening to people (Grammar in a counselling frame)

Short, paired exercises in which person A listens intently to person B in as non-judgemental a way as possible, create a very special atmosphere in a language classroom. Such exercises result in a lowering of defences and an opening-up of people.

Let me illustrate the process by offering you an *anti-counselling* exercise: the students are paired, you ask one of them to prepare to speak for a timed two minutes about a recent holiday. The other person is to listen without interruption. Tell them to use the speaker's words as jumping off points for their own imaginings and speculations; i.e. the opposite of counselling exercises which set out to achieve close attention and listening. The speaker's text is just raw material for them to think out from. After the timed two minutes the 'listener' tells the speaker how she used the speaker's text. The speaker then feeds back her reactions to the listener.

The aim of a *counselling* exercise is for the listener to accurately enter the world of assumption, proposition and feeling of the speaker, bringing in as little of her own judgement and feelings as possible!

And where does grammar come in? If you want students to practise the comparatives (see 'Incomparable', 4.3) put them in threes. One person is to speak for 90 seconds while the other two listen intently. The speaker compares herself to other people she knows, e.g. 'I am more … than my boyfriend, but my sister, Kuniko, is more … than me'. At the end of the 90 seconds the two listeners feed back to the speaker exactly what she said. Each of the three people takes a turn at being the 'comparative' speaker for 90 seconds.

The grammar is being practised in a person-centred atmosphere of concentration on meaning. People are very much in each other's presence and often the speakers are saying important things about themselves.

If you have the right class atmosphere, this counselling section may be just right for your group.

## Section 5  Movement and grammar

All language students need to be asked to get up and do things in the course of their learning. A percentage of people of any age cannot be comfortable unless their periods of stillness are broken up by regular oases of movement.

In this section we offer you games that have people up and moving while practising and internalising grammar, so they are moving but not wasting time. It is in movement that some learners absorb language best, as the movement, the intonation and the grammar form a whole for them. This has been well understood by Suggestopaedic teachers and by Eva Jonai in her work with primary school kids in Hungary.

## Section 6  Meaning and translation

EFL teachers often ask students to make judgements about sounds (ship / sheep) and about grammar (I went / I have gone) in the target language. We rarely ask them to make decisions about meaning, e.g. is 'the train on platform 4 has no wheels' meaningful or nonsense? And yet knowledge about meaning is thrilling to most students even at a low level. As a beginner in Japanese, I get a kick from knowing that the ideas 'spider' and 'cloud' share the sound *kumo*. It is fun to know that the French sentence '*Je suis ce que je suis*' has four meanings (*suis* = I am / *suis* = I follow) 'I am what I am' etc.

This section allows the intermediate to advanced student to play in this area of translation and meaning. So, in 'Iffy sentences' (6.1), the student has to decide whether the sentences she is given are meaningful, iffy, or rubbish. Here are a couple:

Too much is not quite enough
Could I have a little less water in my coffee, please?

A sentence can be propositionally illogical but pragmatically, contextually, apposite.

You may not share our enthusiasm for this area of language and here we enter a plea: even if you don't share the enthusiasm, please try some exercises out with your students to see if **they** do. Teachers often choose exercises they feel easy with but it is a great experiment to try out the odd exercise you don't like. These may bring students in the corner alive in ways you have not witnessed before.

### Section 7  Problem solving

In this section students are asked to find multiple solutions to technical, human and cultural problems and to express themselves within a given set of grammar structures. The kind of thinking involved is the divergent variety, popularised by de Bono.

We first started working grammar this way when confronted with a group of technicians who were learning English. They clearly learnt grammar more willingly when the thinking area was congenial to them. Maybe you, too, have some technically, scientifically minded children/teenagers/adults in your groups?

### Section 8  Correction

In this section you have a mixed bag of correction techniques that you need to select from carefully. Our feeling is that a great deal of correction in language classes flows past the student without having any effect whatsoever. It is part of the teacher's traditional job to correct and if she doesn't correct some students will complain.

We have lots of question marks around this area – here are some of them:

– Who should initiate a correction process: the student who made the mistake, (an)other student/s, the teacher?
– How much does correction or the threat of it, from either inside or out, inhibit and freeze certain students?
– Which students in your class really benefit from direct teacher correction?
– Should you have a correction policy for the whole class or should you treat individuals differently?
– Does it make sense to focus everybody on correctness and accuracy for some part of the lesson as the techniques in this section presuppose?

Here are some caveats about the techniques we propose here:

– Don't use 'Just a minute' (8.1), a boisterous peer correction technique, with a group of students who find it hard to get their sentences out or who culturally hate interrupting others.
– If you use 'Reformulation' (8.3), be aware of the danger of belittling the student by re-expressing her thought too fluently or at a level too high above her own.
– If you use 'Mistakes mirror' (8.4) in which you produce a 'dog' translation of a student's English text, transferring the mistakes to mother tongue, make sure the student in question doesn't feel you are gratuitously making fun of them! This exercise can be a very powerful one.

### Section 9  Presentation

In the mid-nineties there was a great deal of mainstream debate about the usefulness and validity of the lesson plan model that goes thus: presentation – controlled practice – free practice. RSA teacher trainers in the UK wondered whether they should continue to impose this lesson shape, willy-nilly, on their initial trainees.

This final section of the book is in line with such doubts. In 'Listening to time' (9.1) we suggest that intermediate and advanced students can pick useful bits of language from a stream of native speaking speech and then present these patterns to each other. The presentation can then be filled out a bit by the teacher.

In 'Grammar letters' (9.3) we suggest you change presentation channel and introduce new grammar to your students via a 'Dear Everybody' letter. You write your letter in such a way that it is natural for them to practise the same grammar in their answers.

When is presentation quarrying, induction, discovery learning or modelling? Is it useful to distinguish presentation from practice? Is the most effective presentation usually in answer to a student doubt or need?

# Next steps in grammar teaching

As groups of academics and publishers analyse the new (in the mid-nineties) database corpora of spoken English, we are likely to see a new descriptive grammar emerging. This grammar of the spoken language will really put the cat among the EFL teacher pigeons. Will we start prescribing and teaching the features of the spoken language once we can securely identify and describe them? What if they look 'incorrect'? What new techniques and aids will emerge to teach this new oral grammar?

Maybe, good reader, you can now answer all these questions we were asking back in the mid-nineties.

# A note on instructions

You can either explain a game to the students in clear English or else in the students' mother tongue. Even in the mother tongue it can take quite a time to explain and there's often no way of knowing if some or all of the students have misunderstood something until they start playing the game. Students are often in a low energy state at the beginning of a lesson. Also, you might forget or wrongly explain a stage of the instructions, and the instructions for some games can be complicated. We'd like to suggest some alternative ways of starting a game off:

## 1  A short reading comprehension

Write a list of instructions. Either give out the instructions and any other prepared text needed for the game and let the students get on with it, or explain the game once and let the students refer to your written instructions (photocopies, OHP, or on the blackboard) as they play. This is also an excellent, realistic skim reading activity as part of a communicative reading syllabus.

### 2 Picking it up as you go along

Start the game with minimum explanation. Feed in rules and information as you go along; get students who've grasped the rules to explain them to those who haven't. We've found this works well for us and students quickly get used to this way of working.

### 3 'Closed pairs'

This can be done in one of two ways – either you and a student or a group of students start playing the game while the others watch until they pick it up, or you play one half of a 'pair' and the class as a whole play the other half. Do a quick round of the game and then turn it over to pairs/groups of students.

### 4 Dictation

A short dictation at the beginning of a class has always been an excellent way of getting the attention of boisterous or very quiet groups of students. Dictate the rules to the class before beginning to play. A running dictation or dictogloss can be used as an alternative to a straight dictation (see *Dictation*, Davis and Rinvolucri, for these and other alternatives).

Some games lend themselves more to one or other of the presentations above than others.

## *Dedication*

To my wife, Sophie, who supported me through wide mood swings during the writing of *More Grammar Games*.

*Mario*

## 1.1

# Betting on grammar horses

GRAMMAR:  Verbs + *-ing* / verbs + infinitive / verbs that take either

LEVEL:  Upper intermediate

TIME:  30 – 45 minutes

MATERIALS:  Five copies of each of the three **Grammar problem sheets**
Enough copies of each of the three **Grammar answer sheets** to have one per pair of students

THIS GAME CAN BE ADAPTED FOR USE WITH DIFFERENT STRUCTURES AND AT DIFFERENT LEVELS

## In class

1 Ask five students to be the 'horses'; ask them to come and sit at the front of the class facing the others. Tell them you will shortly give them the first **Grammar problem sheet**. Their task will be to reach a *group decision* as to which sentences are correct and which are wrong.

2 Give the rest of the class copies of the first **Grammar answer sheet**. Tell the class not to communicate with the 'horses'.

3 Ask the students to pair off and prepare to lay bets. Each pair has $1000. They must predict how many sentences the 'horses', as a group,

will deal with correctly and *which ones*. If they predict wrongly they lose their money. If they predict correctly, they double their stake. This is the first of three rounds so they shouldn't use all their money. They prepare their bets by ticking the sentences they think the 'horses' will make right judgements about. Each pair shouts out the number of sentences they think the 'horses' will make right judgements about and the amount they are betting, e.g. 'Three correct judgements – we're betting $250.'

4 Now give the 'horses' copies of the first **Grammar problem sheet**. Their task is to decide, as a group, which sentences are correct and which are wrong. The 'horses' discuss in front of the class so that everybody can hear. They make their decision within a four minute time-limit. One of them announces the group decision about each sentence and the rest of the class tells them if they are right or wrong. The 'punters' check their predictions and calculate whether they have lost their money or doubled it. To double their money the 'horses' must have done exactly what they predicted. With some classes it is good to have them shout out, e.g. 'Lost $500!' or 'Doubled $300!'

5 Repeat the betting with two more groups of 'horses' using **Grammar problem sheet 2** and **Grammar problem sheet 3**.

---

### GRAMMAR PROBLEM SHEET 1

1 She dreads coming to class.
2 They delayed issuing the press statement as long as they could.
3 He resents to have to report to the police each day.
4 They can't afford to buy a new car.
5 She promised telling me her secret.

© Cambridge University Press 1995

---

### GRAMMAR PROBLEM SHEET 2

1 She refuses paying up.
2 They enjoy to be praised.
3 Please avoid to use bad language.
4 He forgot buying a ticket.
5 He failed passing the maths exam.

© Cambridge University Press 1995

---

COMPETITIVE GAMES

## GRAMMAR PROBLEM SHEET 3

1 She threatened to make a fuss.
2 He deserves to be shot.
3 He denied eating the last piece of cake.
4 She wishes to ask you a favour.
5 He missed having somebody to dislike.

## GRAMMAR ANSWER SHEET 1

1 She dreads coming to class. **CORRECT**
2 They delayed issuing the press statement as long as
  they could. **CORRECT**
3 He resents to have to report to the police each day. **WRONG**
  *Should be:* **He resents having to report to ...**
4 They can't afford to buy a new car. **CORRECT**
5 She promised telling me her secret. **WRONG**
  *Should be:* **She promised to tell ...**

## GRAMMAR ANSWER SHEET 2

1 She refuses paying up. **WRONG**
  *Should be:* **She refuses to pay up.**
2 They enjoy to be praised. **WRONG**
  *Should be:* **They enjoy being praised.**
3 Please avoid to use bad language. **WRONG**
  *Should be:* **Please avoid using bad language.**
4 He forgot buying a ticket. CORRECT in one meaning,
  WRONG in the other meaning.
  The above sentence means 'He forgot that he had
  bought a ticket'. 'He forgot to buy a ticket' means
  that he forgot that he should buy a ticket.
5 He failed passing the maths exam. **WRONG**
  *Should be:* **He failed to pass the maths exam.**

BETTING ON GRAMMAR HORSES

NOTE

This idea comes from an Italian TV show.

COMPETITIVE GAMES

# 1.2

# Happy grammar families

GRAMMAR: Basic word order
LEVEL: Beginner (monolingual classes)
TIME: 30 – 40 minutes
MATERIALS: One set of **Happy grammar family cards** below per four students
Several pairs of scissors

THIS GAME CAN BE PLAYED AT HIGHER LEVELS TOO, WITH MORE GRAMMATICALLY COMPLEX WORDS BUILT IN, E.G. *AS*, *SINCE*, *AGO*, *WHILE*, *MORE*, ETC.

## Preparation

Photocopy one set of cards below per four students.

## In class

1 Teach the class these words, using translation:
verb
subject
object
article
(The exercise will only work if these concepts are clear to students.) Also pre-teach any unknown words from the sets of cards below.
2 Group the students in fours, two against two, facing each other. Ask them to erect a book barrier on the surface in between them so that pair A cannot see pair B's cards.
3 Give out the sets of cards and scissors. Ask the students to cut the cards out and shuffle them.
4 Explain the rules, using mother tongue:
a) Each pair has five cards – the rest of the cards are in a pool, facing down.
b) The *aim* of the game is to put down as many words as possible in meaningful and grammatically correct sentences. The winners are the pair that have most words in the sentences they have put down by the end of the game. You can also win by getting rid of all the cards in your hand at any point in the game.
c) Pair A start by taking a card from the pool and by asking for a card from pair B. They ask for a grammatical category, e.g. 'Have you got a "subject"?' If the other team have a card in that category and if the

sentence is said in English they must hand it over. Pair A now have seven words and may be able to lay out a sentence.

d) It is now pair B's turn. They take a card from the pool and ask team A for a card etc.

e) During each team's turn they may lay down a sentence if their combination of cards makes it possible. Once a card has been put down as part of a sentence, it is out of the game.

5  As the foursomes play, you may need to further explain the rules and to adjudicate on the correctness of the sentence laid out. The words from the incorrect sentences are returned to the pool.

### ACKNOWLEDGEMENT

We were sent a pack of Pink Elephant Basic Vocabulary cards by a team at the teacher training college in Bialystok, Poland, led by Nancy G. Parker. This Polish team used the 'happy family' frame for lexis – we have used the same frame for grammar.

## HAPPY GRAMMAR FAMILY CARDS

COMPETITIVE GAMES

| VERB | VERB | SUBJECT | SUBJECT |
|------|------|---------|---------|
| can't | have | I | we |

| OBJECT | OBJECT | SUBJECT OR OBJECT | SUBJECT OR OBJECT |
|--------|--------|-------------------|-------------------|
| us | me | you | bread |

| SUBJECT OR OBJECT | SUBJECT OR OBJECT | SUBJECT OR OBJECT | SUBJECT OR OBJECT |
|-------------------|-------------------|-------------------|-------------------|
| CD player | man | woman | car |

| ARTICLE | ARTICLE | ARTICLE | ARTICLE |
|---------|---------|---------|---------|
| a | a | the | the |

## 1.3 | Grammar Reversi

GRAMMAR: Phrasal verbs

LEVEL: Upper intermediate

TIME: 50 minutes

MATERIALS: One set of **Phrasal verb cards**, photocopied and cut up ready for use
Several pairs of scissors
One set of photocopied **Phrasal verb cards** per six students (to be cut up in class by the students)
Envelopes to keep the sets of cards in for later use

THIS GAME CAN BE ADAPTED TO A VARIETY OF STRUCTURES AND CAN BE USED WITH ALL LEVELS

### Preparation

Because the cards have two sides to them, they need careful photocopying. With manual photocopiers, copy side A, noting its position on the glass plate. You take the copied pages and put them face down in the feed tray of the machine so you can copy side B onto the back of side A. Be sure you place your copy of the book on the glass plate in exactly the right position. Check the first photocopy before doing a run!

### In class

1 Gather the class around two threesomes of students and show them how to play the game:

a) Have the two teams sitting opposite each other and deal a pack of 36 **Phrasal verb cards**, giving eighteen to each team.

b) Ask the students to decide which team plays phrasal verbs (the shaded side) and which team plays non-phrasal verbs (the non-shaded side).

c) Show the students the starting position. Each team puts two cards taken at random on the table thus:

| PHRASAL VERB | NON-PHRASAL VERB |
| NON-PHRASAL VERB | PHRASAL VERB |

d) Now ask the phrasal verb team to lay down a phrasal verb card to 'threaten' a non-phrasal verb card:

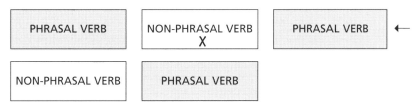

The card marked X is now in danger of being captured (turned over). The phrasal verb team suggests the phrasal verb which corresponds to what's written on the non-phrasal verb side of the card. They check by turning over the card:

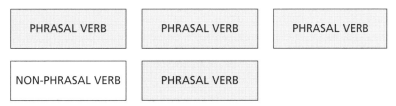

If they're right the card stays turned over. If they're wrong the card is turned back to its original position. (If they don't know the answer they can still turn the card over and have a look for future reference but must replace it in its original position.)

e) Whether they're right or wrong, the non-phrasal verb team now have a turn. They may try to capture card Y like this:

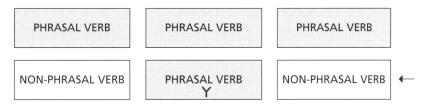

If they give the correct non-phrasal verb 'translation' they can turn Y over like this:

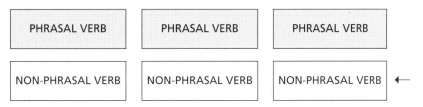

Otherwise they get a look but have to replace the card in its original position.

The basic *rule* is that any card, or sequence of cards of one team which are directly adjacent to each other, can be attacked by being sandwiched between two enemy cards, either horizontally, vertically or diagonally.

The *aim* of the game for the phrasal verb team is to cover the space of the board with their verbs face up. The non-phrasal verb team try to cover the board with 'translations' face up. A player may only lay down a card next to one already on the board, either horizontally, vertically or diagonally.

2  Ask students to imagine that they are playing on a board that is six by six – this makes for a tighter, more interesting game:

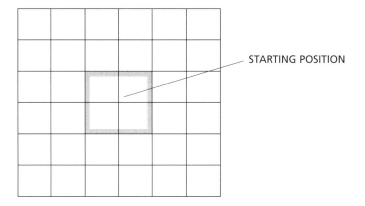

STARTING POSITION

3  Once the students have understood the rules of the game, ask them to break up into groups of six. Each group of six breaks into two teams of three and the threes sit facing each other. Give each group of six the photocopied cards and ask them to fold and tear them or cut them up with the scissors. The students now play the game through. Go from group to group helping with the rules if necessary.

It's worth, at this stage, feeding in an extra rule, group by group, which makes the game more interesting: If a team have sandwiched a sequence of three or more they may capture the whole sequence by getting just two 'translations' right.

COMPETITIVE GAMES

## PHRASAL VERB

*Side A*

1 The dog **went for** him.
2 She hadn't **bargained for** this.
3 It suddenly **dawned on** her.
4 I **feel for** you.
5 She **got over** her illness.
6 The police **looked into** it.
7 He **gave** me the book **back**.
8 They **talked** it **over**.
9 She **did up** her laces.
10 You **wound** them **up**.
11 He **called on** her.
12 She **made for** the living room.
13 He **launched into** a long speech.
14 She **hit on** a brilliant plan.
15 The logo **stands for** the company.
16 This mustn't **come between** us.
17 He **takes after** his mother.
18 They **called** the trip **off**.
19 She **saw** him **off** at the station.
20 He **chatted** her **up**.
21 She **gets on** well **with** him.
22 They **dreamt up** this way of doing it.
23 They **laid on** a good meal.
24 He **jumped at** the idea.
25 He **played down** its importance.
26 They **reeled off** poem after poem.
27 John **brought up** three children.
28 They **put** us **up** for the night.
29 I **bumped into** her at the station.
30 He **put off** his visit.
31 They **pieced together** what happened.
32 She doesn't **hold with** bull-fighting.
33 He **thought up** a solution.
34 She **pulled** his argument **apart**.
35 He was **called up**.
36 She **put** the fire **out**.

## NON-PHRASAL VERB

*Side B*

1 The dog **attacked** him.
2 She hadn't **expected** this.
3 She suddenly **realised**.
4 I **sympathise** with you.
5 She **recovered from** her illness.
6 The police **investigated** it.
7 He **returned** the book to me.
8 They **discussed** it.
9 She **tied** her laces.
10 You deliberately **got** them **cross**.
11 He **visited** her.
12 She **went towards** the living room.
13 He **began** a long speech.
14 She **thought of** a brilliant plan.
15 The logo **symbolises** the company.
16 This mustn't **divide** us.
17 He **is like** his mother.
18 They **cancelled** the trip.
19 She **said goodbye** to him at the station.
20 He **flirted** with her.
21 She **has a good relationship with** him.
22 They **invented** this way of doing it.
23 They **provided** a good meal.
24 He **was really enthusiastic** about the idea.
25 He **minimised** its importance.
26 They **recited** poem after poem.
27 John **raised** three children.
28 They **gave** us **a bed** for the night.
29 I **met** her **by chance** at the station.
30 He **postponed** his visit.
31 They **reconstructed** what happened.
32 She doesn't **agree with** bull-fighting.
33 He **invented** a solution.
34 She **destroyed** his argument.
35 He was **conscripted**.
36 She **extinguished** the fire.

© Cambridge University Press 1995

## Other language you can work on with this game

| *Side 1* | *Side 2* |
|---|---|
| word | its opposite |
| adjective | its comparative form |
| infinitive | irregular past tense |
| target language word | mother tongue equivalent |
| sentence | transformation of sentence (e.g. passive for active or reported speech for direct speech) |

### RATIONALE

This grammar version of Othello or Reversi is a brilliant learning tool as students are constantly being offered a chance to learn and then test themselves. The cards keep being turned over until the very end of the game. Who will win is not clear until very late in the game.
Teaching the class the rules takes a bit of time. Once they have got them clear you can use the game for teaching and testing a great variety of language features.

### NOTE

Since preparing sets of cards for a class of 30 is a long job (you need five sets of 36 cards) it is sensible to delegate this task to some of your students for homework. If you have a class of 30, ask five people to produce a set each – you give them the language they are to put on the cards. Choose people who need extra help with the language area dealt with, as preparing the cards will help them to learn the words or grammar involved.
To satisfy the 'games-players' in your class, give each group a board to play on. The board should have 36 squares on it (6 x 6). This allows players the excitement of edges and corners.

## PHRASAL VERBS 1–12

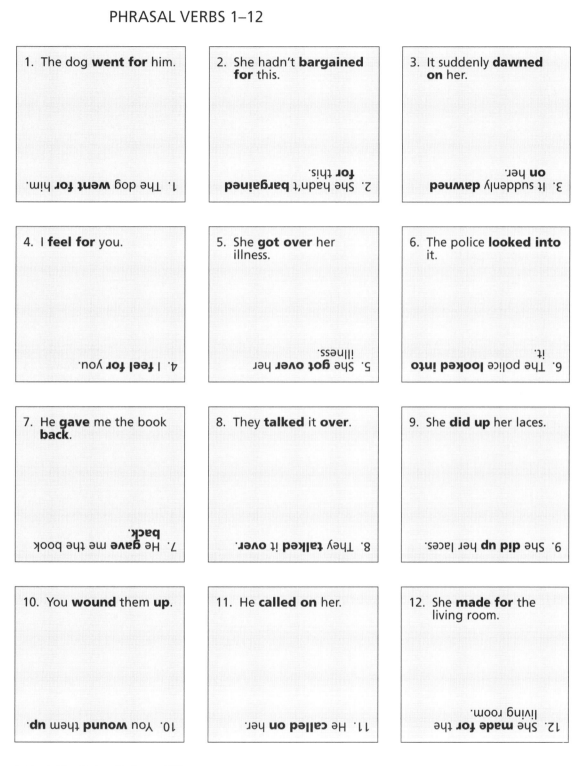

1. The dog **went for** him.

   1. The dog **went for** him.

2. She hadn't **bargained for** this.

   2. She hadn't **bargained for** this.

3. It suddenly **dawned on** her.

   3. It suddenly **dawned on** her.

4. I **feel for** you.

   4. I **feel for** you.

5. She **got over** her illness.

   5. She **got over** her illness.

6. The police **looked into** it.

   6. The police **looked into** it.

7. He **gave** me the book **back**.

   7. He **gave** me the book **back**.

8. They **talked** it **over**.

   8. They **talked** it **over**.

9. She **did up** her laces.

   9. She **did up** her laces.

10. You **wound** them **up**.

    10. You **wound** them **up**.

11. He **called on** her.

    11. He **called on** her.

12. She **made for** the living room.

    12. She **made for** the living room.

GRAMMAR REVERSI

# NON-PHRASAL VERBS 1–12

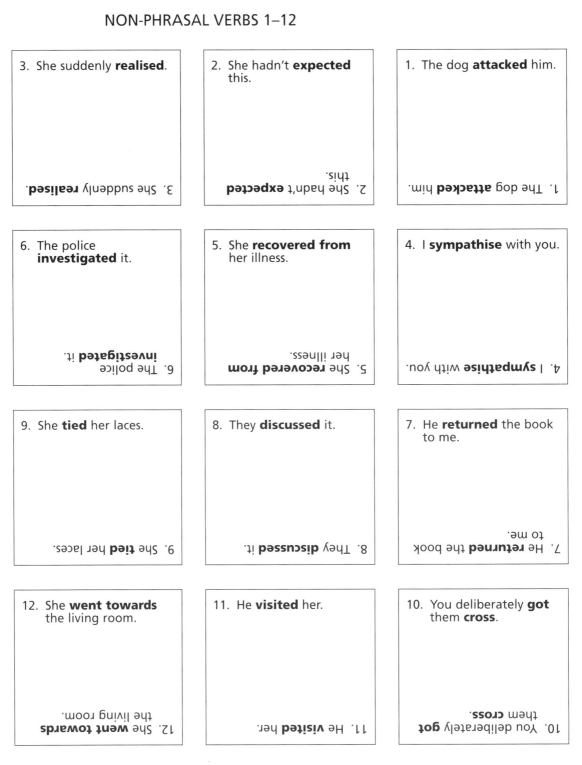

3. She suddenly **realised**.

3. She suddenly **realised**.

2. She hadn't **expected** this.

2. She hadn't **expected** this.

1. The dog **attacked** him.

1. The dog **attacked** him.

6. The police **investigated** it.

6. The police **investigated** it.

5. She **recovered from** her illness.

5. She **recovered from** her illness.

4. I **sympathise** with you.

4. I **sympathise** with you.

9. She **tied** her laces.

9. She **tied** her laces.

8. They **discussed** it.

8. They **discussed** it.

7. He **returned** the book to me.

7. He **returned** the book to me.

12. She **went towards** the living room.

12. She **went towards** the living room.

11. He **visited** her.

11. He **visited** her.

10. You deliberately **got** them **cross**.

10. You deliberately **got** them **cross**.

COMPETITIVE GAMES

## PHRASAL VERBS 13–24

13. He **launched into** a long speech.

13. He **launched into** a long speech.

14. She **hit on** a brilliant plan.

14. She **hit on** a brilliant plan.

15. The logo **stands for** the company.

15. The logo **stands for** the company.

16. This mustn't **come between** us.

16. This mustn't **come between** us.

17. He **takes after** his mother.

17. He **takes after** his mother.

18. They **called** the trip **off**.

18. They **called** the trip **off**.

19. She **saw** him **off** at the station.

19. She **saw** him **off** at the station.

20. He **chatted** her **up**.

20. He **chatted** her **up**.

21. She **gets on** well **with** him.

21. She **gets on** well **with** him.

22. They **dreamt up** this way of doing it.

22. They **dreamt up** this way of doing it.

23. They **laid on** a good meal.

23. They **laid on** a good meal.

24. He **jumped at** the idea.

24. He **jumped at** the idea.

GRAMMAR REVERSI

# NON-PHRASAL VERBS 13–24

15. The logo **symbolises** the company.

15. The logo **symbolises** the company.

14. She **thought of** a brilliant plan.

14. She **thought of** a brilliant plan.

13. He **began** a long speech.

13. He **began** a long speech.

18. They **cancelled** the trip.

18. They **cancelled** the trip.

17. He **is like** his mother.

17. He **is like** his mother.

16. This mustn't **divide** us.

16. This mustn't **divide** us.

21. She **has a good relationship with** him.

21. She **has a good relationship with** him.

20. He **flirted with** her.

20. He **flirted with** her.

19. She **said goodbye** to him at the station.

19. She **said goodbye** to him at the station.

24. He **was really enthusiastic** about the idea.

24. He **was really enthusiastic** about the idea.

23. They **provided** a good meal.

23. They **provided** a good meal.

22. They **invented** this way of doing it.

22. They **invented** this way of doing it.

COMPETITIVE GAMES

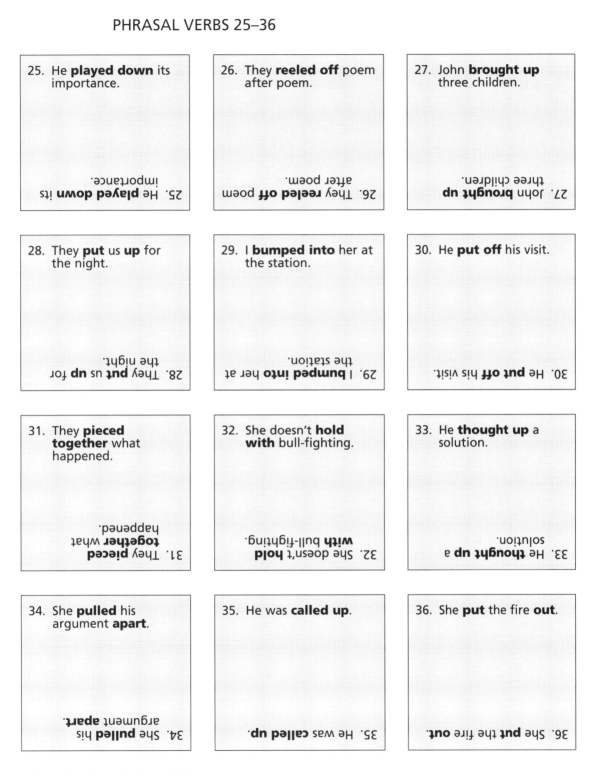

25. He **played down** its importance.

25. He **played down** its importance.

26. They **reeled off** poem after poem.

26. They **reeled off** poem after poem.

27. John **brought up** three children.

27. John **brought up** three children.

28. They **put** us **up** for the night.

28. They **put** us **up** for the night.

29. I **bumped into** her at the station.

29. I **bumped into** her at the station.

30. He **put off** his visit.

30. He **put off** his visit.

31. They **pieced together** what happened.

31. They **pieced together** what happened.

32. She doesn't **hold with** bull-fighting.

32. She doesn't **hold with** bull-fighting.

33. He **thought up** a solution.

33. He **thought up** a solution.

34. She **pulled** his argument **apart**.

34. She **pulled** his argument **apart**.

35. He was **called up**.

35. He was **called up**.

36. She **put** the fire **out**.

36. She **put** the fire **out**.

27. John **raised** three children.

27. John **raised** three children.

26. They **recited** poem after poem.

26. They **recited** poem after poem.

25. He **minimised** its importance.

25. He **minimised** its importance.

30. He **postponed** his visit.

30. He **postponed** his visit.

29. I **met** her **by chance** at the station.

29. I **met** her **by chance** at the station.

28. They **gave** us **a bed** for the night.

28. They **gave** us **a bed** for the night.

33. He **invented** a solution.

33. He **invented** a solution.

32. She doesn't **agree with** bull-fighting.

32. She doesn't **agree with** bull-fighting.

31. They **reconstructed** what happened.

31. They **reconstructed** what happened.

36. She **extinguished** the fire.

36. She **extinguished** the fire.

35. He was **conscripted**.

35. He was **conscripted**.

34. She **destroyed** his argument.

34. She **destroyed** his argument.

COMPETITIVE GAMES

# 1.4

# Three from six grammar quiz

GRAMMAR: Varied
LEVEL: Elementary to advanced
TIME: 15 – 25 minutes
MATERIALS: Set of six questions (for your use only)

## Preparation

Prepare a set of six questions on a grammar area that needs a review. For this game to work the questions should be pretty difficult for the class. The example below was created for an elementary, monolingual class of Arabic speakers:

1 I'll be going to the cinema tonight. Name this tense.
2 Spell the present and past participles of 'to write'.
3 I've been going there ever since I came to Cambridge. Right or wrong?
4 What's the difference between 'hoping' and 'hopping'?
5 What does 'get through' mean? What is it?
6 What's the difference between 'good' and 'well'?

The questions you write need to be too difficult for the individual student but not beyond the combined resources of the class. If you have a large class two or three sets may be necessary.

## In class

1 The aim of the game is for a group to get three questions completely right. Put the class into pairs or small groups. Read out the questions a couple of times to the class (don't write them or let the students take notes as they'll get lots of chances to hear them again as the game progresses).
2 Ask the first group to choose the three they want to attempt out of the six questions. They should say the numbers they want to attempt, e.g. two, five, six. Read out all the questions again on demand as you go along.
3 Read each of the three questions chosen and get the first pair of students to answer them, one by one. When they've given all three answers say how many were right; one out of three, two out of three etc. but don't say which ones were right.

4 Ask the next group to give the numbers of the three they want to answer and repeat the process. As soon as a group gets all three right, discuss and give answers to all six.

## Variation

The format above can also be used to develop reference skills in class. Groups of students have access to grammar books and dictionaries.

### NOTE

We first came across this kind of quiz format on a radio programme. It encourages collaboration and competition at the same time. If the questions are genuinely too difficult for individual students in the class it will take quite a few goes before any one pair gets all three right. The whole class will have listened carefully to each other's answers and explanations and will have thought about the grammar involved.

COMPETITIVE GAMES

# **1.5** Present perfect love story

GRAMMAR: Present perfect simple, continuous, active and passive
LEVEL: Lower intermediate and intermediate
TIME: 40 – 60 minutes
MATERIALS: **Jumbled sentence sheet** on OHP transparency or strips of card
Photocopies of **Unjumbled sentence sheet**

## Preparation

Transfer the **Jumbled sentence sheet** onto an OHP transparency or onto 13 large strips of card that can be read by all the students. Photocopy the **Unjumbled sentence sheet** so you can give them out to each threesome at the end.

## In class

1 Divide the class into teams of three. Tell them they are going to play a grammar game and read a romantic love story at the same time.
2 Explain the task and the scoring:
   a) Students will see a jumbled sentence; they have to sort out the jumble and make a sensible sentence, adding any necessary punctuation.
   b) *Three points* will go to the team that first shouts out an\* unjumbled answer.
   c) Teams that shout out a wrong answer will lose *one point*.
   d) Tell the students that in addition to being jumbled, *three* out of the *thirteen* sentences contain grammar mistakes.
   e) A team that spots a grammar mistake will get *three more points*; if they can put it right they get an additional *two points*.
   f) A team that sees a mistake where there isn't one loses *one point*. (Sentences 7, 11 and 12 are the wrong ones.)
3 Reveal the first jumbled sentence. The first team to call out the unjumbled sentence wins the points. If everybody is stuck then help them by giving the first three words of the sentence in the right order. Allow a maximum of three minutes per sentence. Keep a record of the scores as you go along.
4 Reveal the final scores!
5 Give out the **Unjumbled sentence sheet**.

\* There are obviously other possible correct orders which the students may come up with.

## JUMBLED SENTENCE SHEET

1  I MET MUM HIM AGO TWO MONTHS HIS SISTER AND
2  ME HE I HIM I FANCIED LIKED REALISED TOO REALLY AND
3  FIRST MET MY FRIEND SINCE SHE BEEN 'S WE
4  MORE ME AND HIM HAVE AND MORE EACH OTHER BEEN SEEING OF
5  KIND BEING SO AND GENTLE HE UNDERSTANDING IS
6  TOGETHER SEVERAL TRIPS 'VE BEEN WE ON
7  THERE MINDS SO HE MUCH IF TO TELL YOU BUT 'S I HAVEN ASK'T HIM
8  WELL ACTUALLY WHAT NO WE HAVEN'T THINKING YOU MUST BE DONE
9  UP TRADITIONALLY VERY HE BROUGHT 'S BEEN
10 HOW CAN I PUT A CARDINAL IS THIS HIS DAD
11 GO TO BED ME REFUSED HE IS TO WITH
12 WEEKS TWO SINCE ENGAGED ARE WE
13 WE GETTING NEXT YOU AND DAD COME WEEK 'RE CAN MARRIED

© Cambridge University Press 1995

## UNJUMBLED SENTENCE SHEET

(*other orders than those given here are possible*)

1  Mum, I met him and his sister two months ago.
2  I really fancied him and I realised he liked me too.
3  She's been my friend since we first met.
4  Him and me have been seeing more and more of each other.
5  He is being so kind, gentle and understanding.
6  We've been on several trips together.
7  There's so much to tell you, but I haven't ask**ed** him if he minds.
8  Well, actually, no, we haven't done what you must be thinking!
9  He's been brought up very traditionally.
10 How can I put this … his Dad is a cardinal.
11 He **has** refused to go to bed with me.
12 We **have been** engaged **for** two weeks.
13 We're getting married next week – can you and Dad come?

(sentences 7, 11, 12 have been corrected)

© Cambridge University Press 1995

COMPETITIVE GAMES

NOTE

You can use this technique for lively presentation of any grammar in the coursebook you may be using. Why not get a couple of students to prepare your jumbled sentence OHP transparency for you? There may be times, though, when you have good technical reasons for doing the jumbling yourself. Suppose you have Thai learners who do not hear or pronounce the ends of words, especially consonants, you may want to design the jumbling to focus on endings, e.g. in 9 below:

UP N TRADITIONA VERY... LLY HE BROUGHT'S BEE

(He's been brought up very traditionally.)

# 1.6    Spoof

GRAMMAR:    Example 1: present continuous
Example 2: adjective / noun collocation
LEVEL:    Sheet 1: intermediate
Sheet 2: advanced
TIME:    30 minutes
MATERIALS:    One sheet of sentences per
five students cut onto slips
of paper

YOU CAN PREPARE YOUR OWN
SHEETS OF SENTENCES FOR USE
WITH ALL LEVELS

## Preparation

Write or collect 21 sentences on the grammar area you want to practise.
They should be a mixture of correct and incorrect sentences. Alternatively,
use one of the sheets below if they're appropriate to your class. You need
one sheet per five students. Cut them up so each of the 21 sentences is on a
separate slip of paper.

## In class

1  Group students in fives.* Give each group a set of the 21 sentence slips.
The slips should be placed where everyone in the fivesome can see them.
Tell the students they have ten minutes to discuss whether the sentences
are right or wrong. After the ten minutes give the students time to check
with you. Ask the students not to take notes or mark the slips as the next
stage of the game acts as a review. The slips are then placed face
downwards.
2  Each student should take three slips (six are left over).
3  They can look at their own but not the others' slips. Each student should
guess how many of the fifteen slips that the group have are right or
wrong.
4  Students turn over and display their sentences so that all the group can
see them. They should check which sentences are right and which wrong
and who won by getting the closest guess.
5  Shuffle the slips and have a second round to further reinforce and review
the grammar.

* You may have to have some groups of four.

COMPETITIVE GAMES

## SHEET 1 PRESENT CONTINUOUS

1 He's coming tonight.
2 I'm buying the coffee tomorrow.
3 It's raining later today.
4 I'm dying in 20 years' time.
5 I'm having problems with her.
6 I'm living in Cambridge.
7 If you're coming, I'm coming too.
8 I'm originally coming from Germany.
9 He's always annoying.
10 I'm studying for three years.
11 He's thinking he's wonderful.

12 I'm always living in London.
13 I'm not smoking this weekend.
14 I'm smoking lots of cigars now.
15 I'm not having any money.
16 I'm trying not to think about it.
17 I'm having an opinion about this.
18 I'm having a think about it.
19 I'm seeing to it.
20 I'm going to the cinema on Wednesdays.
21 He's always seeing TV.

NOTE
Sentences 3, 4, 8*, 11*, 12, 15, 17 and 21 are wrong.

## SHEET 2 COLLOCATIONS

1 He's had a heavy meal.
2 They had a heavy conversation.
3 It's light reading.
4 He wants a soft drink.
5 He takes hard drugs.
6 He takes light drugs.
7 She takes soft drugs.
8 He's a weak person.
9 She's a soft person.
10 I only like light music.
11 Let's have soft music.

12 We have soft coffee for breakfast.
13 He smokes soft cigarettes.
14 They serve weak meals.
15 We want a strong coffee.
16 It's only a mild cigarette.
17 There's a strong chance of it happening.
18 There's a light chance of it happening.
19 It's a strong drink.
20 I like mild music.
21 They sell lite cigarettes.

NOTE
Sentences 6, 12, 13, 14, 18 and 20 are not normal collocations.
'Lite' is (American/International) advertising English.

* It is possible to think of circumstances where these would be said by a native speaker. If the students say they are correct, they then need to justify why they are correct.

SPOOF

# 1.7 Student created text

| | |
|---|---|
| GRAMMAR: | Continuous tenses |
| LEVEL: | Intermediate to upper intermediate |
| TIME: | 60 minutes |
| MATERIALS: | One dice per four students Large sheets of blank paper |

THE TEXTS IN THIS ACTIVITY CAN BE ADAPTED FOR USE WITH MANY GRAMMATICAL STRUCTURES AND WITH STUDENTS OF ALL LEVELS

## In class

1 Get the students into groups of four. Choose a grammar area that they are working on at the moment. Ask each student to write, working alone, about six sentences from the grammar area. Three should be right and three wrong; see text below for an example produced by students.

2 The students in their groups then pool their sentences and come up with a definitive list of sixteen, marked right or wrong. They check their list with you. Each student copies the list for the next stage. (The copying phase gives you time to check with all the groups.)

3 Regroup the students: put a pair from one group with a pair from another to make a new group of four. Each student has their own copy of their sixteen-sentence list with them.

4 Ask each group to create a board (16 squares):

| 1 | 2 | 3 | 4 |
|---|---|---|---|
| 8 | 7 | 6 | 5 |
| 9 | 10 | 11 | 12 |
| 16 | 15 | 14 | 13 |

5 Each student gets a coin as a counter and puts it on square 1. Give each group a dice.

6 The first player throws the dice and goes forward to the appropriate square. The opposing pair read a sentence and the player says whether they think it's right or wrong. A *correct* decision takes the player *two forward*, a wrong decision *one back*. The second player from the same team has a turn, followed by the players from the opposing team and so on.
The first pair to both finish win.

## Variation

If the students are preparing for an exam, they can be asked to write examples of multiple choice, gap fill or whatever the format of the exam is.

## Example of a student created text

1 The kids are getting on my nerves.
2 I have been swimming three hours.
3 I am playing tennis a lot lately.
4 I have been looking for it for ages.
5 I am selling my car tomorrow.
6 I am always reading medical books.
7 He is going to have a row.
8 I am dying for a coffee.
9 He is hating that woman.
10 He is always watching his watch.
11 I'm seeing to it.
12 Next year these days I'll have been working as an actor for ten years.
13 I'm trying to forget all about this.
14 I'm having my hair done once a month.
15 I look forward to that party.
16 It rains tonight.

This was made by an upper intermediate class. We found it useful later with an intermediate class.

### NOTE
Sentences 9, 12, and 16 are wrong. Sentences 2 and 14 provoked a lot of discussion about whether they could be right.

# 1.8  Speed

GRAMMAR:   Collocations with *wide*, *narrow* and *broad*
LEVEL:      Intermediate to advanced
TIME:       15 – 20 minutes
MATERIALS:  Three cards, with *wide* on one, *narrow* on the second and *broad* on the third

YOU CAN CREATE YOUR OWN MATERIAL FOR LOWER LEVELS USING DIFFERENT COLLOCATIONS

## Preparation

Prepare three large cards with *wide* on one, *narrow* on the second and *broad* on the third.

## In class

1  Clear as much space as you can in your classroom so that students have access to all the walls and ask two students to act as secretaries at the board. Stick each of your cards on one of the other three walls of the room. Ask the rest of the students to gather in the middle of the space.

2  Tell the students that you are going to read out sentences with a word missing. If they think that the right word for that sentence is *wide* they should rush over and touch the *wide* card. If they think the word should be *narrow* or *broad* they touch the respective card instead. Tell them that in some cases there are two right answers (they choose either).

3  Tell the secretaries at the board to write down the correct versions of the sentences in full as the game progresses.

4  Read out the first gapped sentence and have the students rush to what they think is the appropriate wall. Give the correct version and make sure it goes up on the board. Continue with the second sentence etc.

5  At the end of the strenuous part ask the students to take down the sentences in their books. A relief from running!
(If the students want a challenge they should get a partner and together write down as many sentences as they can remember with their backs to the board before turning round to complete their notes. Or else have their partner dictate the sentence with a 'gap' for them to try to complete.)

COMPETITIVE GAMES

## SENTENCES TO READ OUT

| | Key |
|---|---|
| They used a .......... angled lens. | WIDE |
| He looked at her with a .......... smile. | BROAD |
| The Socialists won by a .......... margin. | NARROW / BROAD |
| She is very .......... minded. | BROAD / NARROW |
| He speaks the language with a .......... London accent. | BROAD |
| Everybody was in .......... agreement. | BROAD |
| You were wrong – what you said was .......... of the mark. | WIDE |
| You had a .......... escape. | NARROW |
| Of course they are .......... open to criticism. | WIDE |
| They went down the canal in a .......... boat. | NARROW |
| She opened her eyes .......... . | WIDE |
| The news was broadcast nation........... | WIDE |
| The path was three metres .......... . | WIDE |
| The light was so bright that she .......... her eyes. | NARROWED |

## Variation

You can play this game with many sets of grammar exponents:
– forms of the article; *a*, *the* and zero article
– prepositions
etc.

### ACKNOWLEDGEMENT

We learnt this game structure from George Tunnell, writing in *PET*, March 1993.

## 1.9

# I challenge

GRAMMAR: Word endings and suffixes (e.g. *-s / -ed / -ing / -er*)
LEVEL: Beginner to elementary
TIME: 25 minutes
MATERIALS: None

## In class

The aim of the game is to avoid completing a word yourself and to force someone else into completing it later.

1 Ask a student to call out a letter. It should be the first letter of a word she can visualise. Write the letter on the board.

2 Ask the student next to her to call out a letter. Write it immediately after the first one. Continue with the next student in line and so on.

3 The student whose turn it is can call out 'I challenge' instead of a letter. A challenge can be because no possible addition of a letter / letters will make an English word. If the student who provided the last letter can suggest a word, the challenge is defeated. The round is over.

The other grounds for a challenge is that the letters on the board already make a word. This challenge can be defeated if the student who is being challenged can make a *longer* word which they say out loud. The round is over. Start a new sequence.

4 After a few words done round the class the exercise can be done by the students in small groups.

## Example

Challenge 1: The first four students produce 'gree'. The next student challenges but can be defeated by student 4 suggesting 'greed'.

Challenge 2: The first five students produce 'red'. The next student can challenge because this is a complete word. Student 5 can defeat the challenge by saying 'reddish', 'redder' etc.

## Variation 1

Ask students to choose whether their letter is added before or after the letter sequence on the board.

COMPETITIVE GAMES

## Variation 2

Ask students to add any letters and to resequence the ones already on the board in response to a challenge.

### NOTE

This game concentrates students' attention on word endings -*s*, -*ed*, -*ing*, -*er* etc. and word building. In languages which have more inflexions than English, it is an even more valuable exercise.

### ACKNOWLEDGEMENT

Thanks to Issam Al Khayyat for suggesting this exercise and to Jeanne McCarten for variation 2.

# The triangle game

| | |
|---|---|
| GRAMMAR: | Prepositions |
| | Adverbs of time, place and movement |
| LEVEL: | Intermediate and above |
| TIME: | 40 – 50 minutes |
| MATERIALS: | One large card triangle and three strips of paper per nine students |

## Preparation

Cut out one large card triangle and three strips of paper for each group of nine students.

## In class

1 Dictate this list of adverbs and prepositions:

| | | |
|---|---|---|
| on foot | during | by |
| by bus | opposite | across |
| for | nowhere | through |
| until | upstream | in and out |
| around | apart | downtown |
| overseas | upstairs | ashore |
| high up | southward | beyond |
| among | near | between |
| next door | aboard | next to |
| on top of | past | on |
| into | in | |

Ask students to check with their neighbours that they haven't missed or misspelt any words and check unknown words. Help them if necessary.

2 Arrange the students into groups of approximately nine people round tables and give each group one of the card triangles and three strips of paper. Ask them to write these words on the strips of paper and place them in the angles of the triangle: *place*, *time* and *movement*.

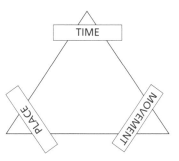

PROBLEM SOLVING

3 Within each group of nine, three sit near the *place* angle, three near the *time* angle and three near the *movement* angle.

4 Tell them how the game works:

   a) The first team chooses one of the dictated words which they think won't fit in their corner. They write it on a slip of paper and place it in the most appropriate corner.

   b) The team in that corner has 25 seconds to produce a correct sentence showing the word used in their corner's meaning.* If they manage to do this they get a point. If they can't they may challenge the first team to give them a sentence with that meaning. If the first team can't do so then they lose a point (they get minus one).

   c) The team who have just played lay down a new word, but *not* in their own corner.

5 Get the students playing simultaneously in their tables of nine. Hover between the tables and act as referee for the correctness of the sentences produced.

6 Draw the game to a close just before the energy begins to flag and handle any language problems arising.

He has gone **past** the pub.

* The sentence must show the *place*, *time* or *movement* meaning of the preposition or adverb, e.g. 'They went **ashore**' clearly shows the *movement* function of **ashore**.
If 'past' has been placed in the *movement* corner then the following sentence does *not* illustrate movement: 'They were standing just **past** the pub' while this sentence does: 'He has gone **past** the pub, call him back'.

THE TRIANGLE GAME

# 2.1

# One becomes two

| | |
|---|---|
| GRAMMAR: | Varied syntax and grammar; strong focus on punctuation and therefore on stress and intonation |
| LEVEL: | Elementary to advanced |
| TIME: | 20 – 30 minutes |
| MATERIALS: | None |

## In class

1 Tell the students you want them to expand a short sentence into two utterances by adding one or two words, e.g.

It happened a week ago.

might become:

It happened. *They knew* a week ago.

2 Explain the rules to the students:
   a) The original sequence of words must not be altered except by the addition of one or two words; not more than two.
   b) The first of the two new sentences must end with a colon, full stop, question mark or exclamation mark. Students are free to change punctuation.

3 Tell the students to make as many two-sentence pairs as they can from the head sentence 'It happened a week ago'. Go round and check that everybody has understood the rules. Help students with grammatically 'illegal' sentences.

4 Ask the students to work in small groups and compare their sentences and the contexts in which they would make sense.

5 Ask each small group to pick the sentence pairs they most like and to put these up on the board to share with the rest of the class. Students are often amazed at other people's creativity.

## Example

One upper intermediate group came up with these sentences:
It happened. *Yes, actually*, a week ago.
It happened a week ago? *Not likely!*
It happened *twice* a week. *Years* ago.
It happened *to me*. A week ago.

It *never* happened. *Just* a week ago?
*Did* it? *Really* happened a week ago?
It happened. A week ago *last Thursday*.
It *was found*. Happened a week ago.
It *only* happened *once*. A week ago.
*Yes*, it happened. *A terrible* week ago.
It happened *once* a week. *Long* ago.
*I saw:* It happened a week ago.
'It happened', *she said*. 'A week ago'.
It happened? *What happened* a week ago?

## Variation

Here are more head sentences that have worked well:

Never again!
You're rather fed-up, aren't you?
We have been thinking about them recently.
Well, actually, I had intended to.
Do please come round and see us.

### RATIONALE

This exercise, like those in Section II of *Grammar Games*, gives learners space and time to explore grammar and syntax possibilities and restrictions. As with most things that derive from the work of Caleb Gattegno, it is fiercely cognitive and loads of fun. Some of the mathematically minded people in your class are likely to find the exercise very stimulating.

### NOTE

You may want to show the example sentences to the students after they have written their own and this could have the effect of leading them into areas they had not seen for themselves. However, we would not advise this as we have found with this activity it is more exciting for the students to discover what they discover without reference to the work of other groups.

## 2.2 Mind-reading

GRAMMAR: Varied
LEVEL: Beginner to intermediate
TIME: 20 – 30 minutes
MATERIALS: None

## In class

1 Ask each student to draw a part of something, e.g. a man with a dog on a lead but omitting the dog. They exchange drawings with a partner and complete each other's *without* communicating. If the completion is roughly what the initial artist intended the completer gets a point.

2 Give the students a topic to write on, e.g. bungee-jumping, hens, clouds, overtime, catching a cold. Tell each student to write a five to eight word sentence about one of the topics on a slip of paper and then tear off the last two or three words. Each student then gives the first part of the sentence to their partner for completion. The completer gets one point for correctly reading the mind of the writer and two points for picking up on any mistakes made by the writer. (At this stage you will be haring round the room judging sentences.)

3 Change the pairings and repeat the exercise but don't overdo it.

## Variation

Instead of asking students to chop off the last two or three words of their sentence, experiment with asking them to omit other parts of the sentence, e.g. the first two words, all the nouns, all the verbs, the one word they consider most important in the sentence etc.

### RATIONALE

The linguistic sophistication of this exercise is considerable. Students are working simultaneously on likely meanings, on grammar and on the ways words come together (collocation). *They* are doing the mental work, mostly unconsciously, and the teacher is in role as a sounding board and this only on demand: pure Silent Way.

### ACKNOWLEDGEMENT

We learnt this exercise from a seven-year-old, Bruno Rinvolucri.

COGNITIVE GAMES

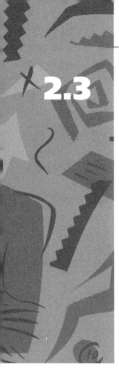

## 2.3    Weed-read

| | |
|---|---|
| GRAMMAR: | Varied |
| LEVEL: | **Text for weeding 1:** lower intermediate |
| | **Text for weeding 2:** advanced |
| TIME: | 15 – 25 minutes |
| MATERIALS: | One **Text for weeding** per pair of students |

YOU CAN USE THIS IDEA TO PRODUCE YOUR OWN TEXTS FOR USE WITH DIFFERENT LEVELS

## In class

1  Give the students a text with distractor words you've peppered in, or use **Text for weeding 1** or **Text for weeding 2** (below). Ask them to work in pairs and weed out the extra words.
2  Ask the students to compare their work in groups of six.
3  Dictate the list of 'weeds'.

---

### TEXT FOR WEEDING 1

*Please take out the eight words or phrases that are extra to the text below.*

#### Letters or litter

A foreign, alien student was in London attending to a language school. She knew little English and had no one to talk to.

She wrote a also lot of letters to her family back home. Over the bridge three weeks she wrote a total of twenty letters.

No one didn't wrote to her. Finally she rang absolutely home. Her mother was furious. She said she had received no letters. The girl could not understand what had not happened. When she was going to post her twenty-first letter she saw the word of God on the box: *litter*!

© Cambridge University Press 1995

---

**37**

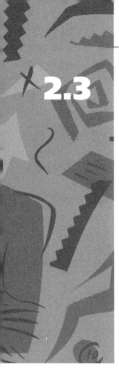

## LIST OF EIGHT TEXT WEEDS (for dictation)

alien   to   also   the bridge   didn't   absolutely   not   of God

---

### TEXT FOR WEEDING 2

*Please take out the fifteen words or phrases that are extra to the text below. The first word, 'the', needs to come out, for example.*

### *Doom seen in crumbling of chopstick culture*

The Japanese children are becoming so as undisciplined and used to be sloppy Western ways of eating that barely more than ten per cent of primary school pupils up the ladder to the age of ten know how to use chopsticks properly and rudely.

A new survey has been alarmed traditionalists. The inability to use chopsticks, they say, not in addition only shows poor manners, but demonstrates declining parental discipline and bodes ill and disease for Japan's economic future.

The survey showed that among children up between to the age of ten, a mere huge 10.6 per cent could use chopsticks in the approved manner. Among older children there was some improvement but not much more. By mistake contrast, a 1936 study found some stupid 75 per cent of infants aged three-and-a-half could use chopsticks: today the figure is less interesting than one per cent.

(from *The Guardian*, 10 June 1992)

---

## LIST OF FIFTEEN TEXT WEEDS (for dictation)

the   as   be   more than   the ladder   and rudely   been
in addition   and disease   between   huge   more   mistake   stupid
interesting

COGNITIVE GAMES

## Variation

Ask one of your groups to plant weeds in texts for another of your groups. Some students seem to prefer weeding while others enjoy text-twisting. Both versions of the exercise focus well on both meaning and grammar. This variation is a good exercise for a class to do in a word-processing room.

### RATIONALE

Pulling out the weeds in a choked garden tests your recognition of plants. Similarly, in this exercise, students are testing their knowledge of collocation, grammar and syntax by throwing out the intruders.

### ACKNOWLEDGEMENT

We learnt this exercise from Jim Brims who came across it when he was sitting the UK Civil Service exams. (The exercise is used in some of the higher UCLES EFL exams.)

# 2.4

# Don't 'she' me*

| | |
|---|---|
| GRAMMAR: | Word-building |
| LEVEL: | Intermediate to advanced |
| TIME: | 45 minutes |
| MATERIALS: | None |

## In class

1 Get your students to brainstorm parts of the body.

2 Ask the students, working in groups, to add the suffix -ed to each of the nouns and see which can be made into verbs. Ask them to make sentences to illustrate the meanings of the verbs. They can use dictionaries. You are likely to get sentences like these:

He **head**ed south.

They **eye**d the cake.

The car **nose**d out.

(Some names for parts of the body cannot be made into full verbs, e.g. wrist, femur.)

He **headed** the ball

3 Bring the class back together and discuss the meanings, helping where necessary.

* It's often thought rude to say 'he' or 'she' to refer to someone who's present. Someone objecting to this might easily say 'Don't she me.' Even he or she can be verbed in English.

COGNITIVE GAMES

## Variation 1

Choose another set of nouns that can mostly be turned into verbs. For example, give the students a picture of a building site and elicit concrete nouns like the following: brick, floor, plaster, pipe, roof, nail, felt, tile. Picture dictionaries are a good source of nouns that can be turned directly into verbs.

## Variation 2

Ask the students to come up with a collection of any short, concrete nouns and see how many of them can be turned directly into verbs. The conversion-into-verb rate with a random collection of short concrete nouns seems to be around 50 per cent, e.g. road (–), ship (+), land (+), mother (+), cousin (–), pan (+), cow (+), turkey (–), fox (+), owl (–), knife (+), car (–), picture (+), garden (+), wood (–), oven (–).

### RATIONALE

One feature of English is that is is an intensely 'verbed' language – 'The spirit of English is verbs' (Gattegno). It's worth the students getting an insight into this fact.

### ACKNOWLEDGEMENT

John Morgan invented this exercise.

## 2.5 Final word

| | |
|---|---|
| GRAMMAR: | Word position in the sentence |
| LEVEL: | Intermediate |
| TIME: | 30 – 40 minutes |
| MATERIALS: | None |

> THIS ACTIVITY CAN BE ADAPTED TO SUIT ALL LEVELS

## In class

1  Split the class into mixed ability groups of three. Explain that they will be writing sentences against the clock. Tell them each sentence must end with a word from a sentence you give them. For example, if the sentence is:

**With great difficulty we managed to open the rear door of the plane.**

ask them to write thirteen sentences, each sentence is to end with a different word from the sentence, e.g.:

Who are you going to the party **with**?

That was **great**.

Tell them they have ten minutes to write the thirteen sentences. Time the exercise and tell them after three, six and nine minutes. This gets the adrenalin going. The winning team will be the one that manages the largest number of grammatically correct sentences, each of which uses a different word from the head sentence and uses it in final position. They must do all this within the ten minute time-limit.

During the writing phase give *no help* other than going round ticking correct sentences. (To be correct the sentence must end in a word from the head sentence *and* be in itself grammatically acceptable.) If you give any help to one team beyond ticking good sentences, you have to give equal help elsewhere, which kills the game.

2  When the time is up ask the teams to read out any sentences you have not been able to tick. (With a class of 40 you will have had around 100 sentences to monitor in ten minutes – few teams write all thirteen sentences in the time.) When the students read out their sentences just say 'right' or 'wrong'.

3  The teams add up their scores so a winner and runner-up emerge.

4  Get each team to write up one wrong sentence on the board. The students have a chance to correct each other's mistakes.

COGNITIVE GAMES

5 Get the whole class to tackle any 'end words' they could not find sentences for, e.g.:
The word I'd use is '**the**'.
He just said '**the**'.
6 Round off the lesson by asking the teams to put up on the board one sentence they've written that they really like.

## Variation

Do the exercise as above but ask the students to use the words from the head sentence in different positions in their sentences, e.g. in initial position:
**With** you I feel good.
**Great** to see you.
**Difficulty** lies in the eyes of the beholder.
You could also usefully get them to use second position, e.g.
Living **with** granny is hard.
and penultimate position, e.g.
I agree **with** you.

## 2.6

# DIY* word order

GRAMMAR: Word order
LEVEL: Beginner to advanced
TIME: 15 – 25 minutes
MATERIALS: Any text

## Preparation

Select a text.

## In class

1 Ask the students to skim the text and to choose their favourite word. Ask some of them to say their words to the group and explain why they like them.
2 Ask each student to secretly choose their favourite sentence from the text. They then cut or fold and tear a piece of paper into enough oblongs to be able to write each word (including punctuation) on a separate piece.

* DIY = do-it-yourself (home improvements).

COGNITIVE GAMES

3 Each student mixes up the pieces and places them on their chair. Students then mill around, choose a chair and reconstruct the sentence on it. Remind them to remix the pieces before moving on. Stop them when they've done half a dozen sentence reconstructions.

## Variation 1

Ask the students to add an extra, irrelevant word to their sentence. When other students reconstruct the sentence they omit the dummy word.

## Variation 2

Ask the students to leave a word out of their sentences and to include a blank bit of paper to stand for the missing word. When other students reconstruct the sentence they need to include the missing word but *not* to write it on the blank slip of paper.

### NOTE

This exercise works well with any text and will get people actively involved, even with poor texts.

### ACKNOWLEDGEMENT

The exercise was shown to us by Jonathan Marks, co-author with Tim Bowen of *The Pronunciation Book*.

# 2.7 Body tense map

| | |
|---|---|
| GRAMMAR: | Tenses and their uses |
| LEVEL: | Elementary to advanced |
| TIME: | 30 – 45 minutes |
| MATERIALS: | Large sheets of paper |

## In class

1 Brainstorm all the names of the tenses that the class know and their main uses with an example of each. Write them on the board.
So, for *present continuous* you might have:

**Now** (present), e.g. We're having a look at the tenses.
**Now** (temporary), e.g. I'm living in London at the moment.
**Future reference**, e.g. I'm moving house next year.

Students may want to name the tenses by giving examples, e.g. *used to* rather than 'habitual past'.

2 If the group is an elementary one you may end up with half a dozen tense uses. At a higher level you will find they have come up with many tense uses, maybe including conditionals and the infinitive.

3 Create as much space as possible by moving furniture to the sides of the room. In the next step the students will each be asked to represent a tense use with their bodies. If you have a class of 30 and you have thirteen or fourteen tense uses, divide the class into two groups of fifteen so each student has a tense use to represent. Each of the two groups take half the space available to prepare their tense tableaux. Depending on the number in the class and the number of tense uses brainstormed, decide on the groupings needed in your particular class.

4 Now ask the students, in their groups, to represent the relationships between the verb tense uses spatially, using their bodies. So you may find a *past continuous* student standing with arms outstretched behind the *simple past* one, if they have recently come across a pattern like 'He dropped in while I was working'. A *past perfect* student might be reaching out to touch the shoulder of the *past tense* student.

5 Your role in this exercise is to listen to the students' discussions and doubts and to intervene as little as possible.

6 If there are several groups in the room, ask each group to explain its special organisation to you and the others.

COGNITIVE GAMES

If you are working with the class as one group, ask each tense use to explain why they are standing, sitting or lying as and where they are.

7 Give out large sheets of paper so that the students can record their spatial representations of the tenses. Encourage the use of colour.

By now you will have gathered lots of useful diagnostic information.

## NOTE 1

Plenty of EFL books present the tenses in timeline fashion. This can lead to odd ideas like thinking that the *present perfect* is somehow closer in time to *now* than the simple past:

I've been religious ever since I can remember.

She popped in a minute ago.

If you present the exercise above to the students as one in which they produce whatever tableaux they want of the tenses, they sometimes come up with interesting alternatives to and variations on the timelines often presented in EFL books.

## NOTE 2

In primary classrooms, children who learn by doing, the very kinaesthetic ones, spend plenty of time in their preferred mode. This is not usually the case in secondary and adult classrooms. This exercise is highly kinaesthetic and will come as a relief to people who learn best this way. In step 7 the visual folk get their turn!

BODY TENSE MAP

## 2.8 Shunting words

| | |
|---|---|
| GRAMMAR: | Mainly syntax, especially clause coordination |
| LEVEL: | Elementary to advanced |
| TIME: | 20 – 40 minutes |
| MATERIALS: | Prepared text typed into a word processor |

## Preparation

Type into your word processor a text that the group has already read and find fairly hard. Then remove all the punctuation and all the spaces between the words so that you get a text looking like this:

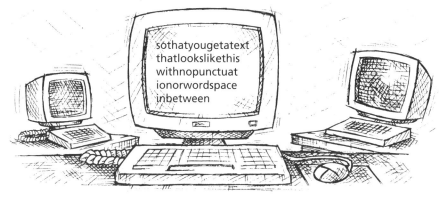

sothatyougetatext
thatlookslikethis
withnopunctuat
ionorwordspace
inbetween

## In the computer room

1 You can have up to three students round each computer – ideally you will have one computer per student as most people prefer to word-process on their own, if there is a choice.
2 Tell the students to space and punctuate the text.
3 Go round and help with things they can't sort out and explain words they don't know.

### RATIONALE

This is a linguistically thrilling Computer Assisted Language Learning (CALL) exercise that has people working on at least these areas:
– word segmentation (*theshortwords* are the hardest to separate)
– seeing or hearing clauses

- focus on syntax, punctuation and meaning
- inevitable intensive reading (Japanese lower intermediate students, who sometimes sank into passivity when confronted with hard text, sprang into active life when we tried this with them)
- an active, editorial attitude to text

The students only need minimal word processing skills to do this exercise efficiently – language learning time is not wasted on word processing technicalities.

## NOTE

The second time you use this exercise ask a word processing efficient student to prepare the exercise for the rest of the class. Involving students in the preparation of class material is one of the central concepts in *Lessons from the Learners*, by Sheelagh Deller.

## ACKNOWLEDGEMENT

We came across the running-words-together technique in *Alternatives* by Richard and Majorie Baudains. They could have got it from early Latin scripts that do not mark word boundaries with spaces. Their exercise is best done on a word processor.

SHUNTING WORDS

# Mending sentences

| | |
|---|---|
| GRAMMAR: | Varied |
| LEVEL: | Post beginner to advanced |
| TIME: | 20 – 30 minutes |
| MATERIALS: | Prepared chosen sentence |

## Preparation

Choose a sentence that illustrates grammar you are currently working on with the group.
Suppose the sentence is:

**New shoes hurt my feet**

then rewrite the sentence four times this way:

**Shoes new hurt my feet** (word 1 goes into second position)
**New hurt shoes my feet** (word 2 goes into third position)
**New shoes my hurt feet** (word 3 goes into fourth position)
**New shoes hurt feet my** (word 4 goes into fifth position)

## In Class

1 Put the sentence up on the board with the four rewrites.
2 Put the students into teams of three, with team A facing team B and team C facing team D etc.
   The task of each team of three is to try and make the rewritten sentences grammatically correct *with as few changes as possible*. (The change can be altering words morphologically, adding in new words as well as altering punctuation. Students are *not* allowed to delete words.) The teams facing each other are in competition with one another and with all the teams in the room. Give them a time-limit of five minutes per sentence.
3 Explain the scoring system:
   – one point off for each morphological change
   – one point off for each word added
   – one point off for each change in punctuation
   – three points off if the sentence proposed is bad English
   The aim of the game is to run up the lowest possible negative score. Each

team keeps their own score. They appeal to you over the correctness of their new sentences if challenged by the team opposite.

Here are three possible rewrites of **Shoes new hurt my feet**:

Shoes ... new ones hurt my feet.

Shoes, when new, hurt my feet.

The shoes are new and hurt my feet.

If a team writes number 1 or 2 above, they have introduced two changes (a new word and changed punctuation) and so get two negative points. If a team writes number 3 above, they have introduced three changes and so get three negative points.

4 Having used **Shoes new hurt my feet** to show the class how the game works, ask them to move onto **New hurt shoes my feet**. Remind them of the five-minute time-limit.

5 They tackle the last two rewrites.

6 At the end of the game ask the teams to shout out any sentences where they are not sure about the grammar. Put them up on the board and give a judgement on each of them. With this information in hand ask the teams to add up their scores so that a winner and runner-up emerge.

# 2.10 Hinged sentences

GRAMMAR: Syntax and punctuation
LEVEL: Intermediate
TIME: 20 – 30 minutes
MATERIALS: One **Hinged sentences** sheet per two students

THIS ACTIVITY CAN BE ADAPTED FOR USE WITH STUDENTS FROM INTERMEDIATE TO ADVANCED LEVEL

## In class

1 Give out the **Hinged sentences** sheet and ask the students to scan through for any that make sense as they stand. (sentences 3, 5, 11)

2 Students work in pairs or alone and rewrite each of the twelve sentences into two separate sentences that share a hinge word or phrase, adding necessary punctuation and capitals etc. Give this example:

He loves her children are great = He loves **her**. / **Her** children are great.

In this case **her** is the 'hinge' word.

In many of the sentences there is more than one possible hinge word or phrase, e.g. sentence 6 below can become:

Read **this** – **this** sentence is an example of ambiguity. or:

Read **this sentence** – **this sentence** is an example of ambiguity.

---

### HINGED SENTENCES

1 I love his face is very unlovable.
2 Please don't do that is just what we must do.
3 I think I understand your feeling is not at all clear to me.
4 Who has taken my scissors are there on the table.
5 I wanted to tell you this is something I can't tell you.
6 Read this sentence is an example of ambiguity.
7 Don't get there too late husbands are a matter of regret.
8 Prices are on the up and up yours said the man.
9 Do you really have to go so soon is not that polite.
10 Tell me what you'd like to do whatever you like.
11 I feel you understand nothing at all.
12 I believe in yesterday couldn't have been better.

© Cambridge University Press 1995

---

COGNITIVE GAMES

## Variation 1

This sentence manipulation technique works well in getting students to focus on particle verbs, e.g.:
He took his shoes **off** to the beach they went.
He put them **up** on the top shelf is where she put them.

## Variation 2

Ask students to create their own 'hinged sentences' in English and in mother tongue.

### ACKNOWLEDGEMENT
We have brought this technique over from the 'Milton Erickson model' widely used in Neuro-Linguistic Programming style trance inductions.

# Spot the differences

| | |
|---|---|
| GRAMMAR: | Common mistakes |
| LEVEL: | Elementary |
| TIME: | 20 – 30 minutes |
| MATERIAL: | One copy of **Late-comer A** and **Late-comer B** for each student |

THIS ACTIVITY CAN BE ADAPTED
FOR USE WITH ALL LEVELS

## In class

1 Pair the students and give them the two texts. Ask them to spot all the differences they can between them. Tell them that there may be more than one pair of differences per pair of parallel sentences. Tell them one item in each pair of alternatives is correct.
They are to choose the correct form from each pair.

2 Ask them to dictate the correct text to you at the board. Write down *exactly* what they say, so students have a chance to correct each other both in terms of grammar and in terms of their pronunciation. If a student pronounces *dis voman* for 'this woman' then write up the wrong version. Only write it correctly when the student pronounces it right. Your task in this exercise is to allow the students to try out their hypotheses about sound and grammar without putting them right too soon and so reducing their energy and blocking their learning. Being too kind can be cognitively unkind.

COGNITIVE GAMES

## LATE-COMER A

This women was often very late.
She was late for meetings.
She were late for dinners.
She was late when she went to the cinema.
One day she arrive for a meeting half an hour early.
Nobody could understand because she was early.
'Of course,' someone said, 'clocks put back last night'.

© Cambridge University Press 1995

## LATE-COMER B

This woman was often very late.
She was late for meeting.
She was late for dinners.
She was late as she went to the cinema.
One day she arrived for meeting half an hour early.
Nobody couldn't understand why she was early.
'Of course,' someone say, 'the clocks were put back last night'.

## Variation

To make this exercise more oral, pair the students and ask them to sit facing each other. Give **Late-comer A** to one student and **Late-comer B** to the other in each pair. They then have to do very detailed listening to each other's texts.

### NOTE

If you are teaching a class that shares the same mother tongue, the way to use this exercise is to take a bit of student-produced text and rewrite it as two 'spot the differences' texts. You put some of the student's mistakes in one text and some in the other.

# Self-generated language

GRAMMAR: Varied
LEVEL: Post beginner to elementary
TIME: 30 – 50 minutes
MATERIALS: 20 – 30 small squares of different coloured cardboard

## Preparation

Cut out 20 – 30 small squares of cardboard of varying colours and sizes.

## In class

1 Ask for a volunteer to tell a story about themselves to the group. It may take a moment for a teller to emerge. The teller may speak in English or in a mixture of mother tongue and English.

2 Ask the teller to take the pile of coloured squares and to put one up where the class can see it after saying each sentence of their story. The coloured square from then on represents that sentence.

3 Sit behind the teller. Ask the teller to begin. After each sentence you repeat it in a form as close to the teller's as possible. You give a helpful counselling reformulation, rather than a teacherly correction. When the teller has said three or four sentences, stop them and point to one of the three or four coloured squares. Either the teller or someone in the group repeats the sentence represented by the card you are pointing to. Ask the teller to go on. After two or three more sentences you ask someone to recap from the beginning.

4 When the teller has finished the story, ask students to point to cards they remember and to say what they can bring back to mind. Each student may work from one card only, so there is sharing rather than people with good memories monopolising.

### Variation

1 At the beginning of a lesson divide the class into small groups, give out copies of the **Instructions sheet** below, together with sets of 20 – 30 square cards. Leave the room for a good 30 minutes. It's important to resist the temptation to keep popping back. You may want to rewrite the handout half in mother tongue and half in English, if the class level is

COGNITIVE GAMES

very low. (Mixed language text is very useful with beginners, e.g.: Please *lesen* these *Instruktionen*.)

---

## INSTRUCTIONS SHEET

1 Please read these instructions.
2 Choose a leader. The leader will organise your work.
3 Choose a story-teller. The story-teller will tell a personal story or describe a place.
4 Give the coloured squares to the story-teller. They produce a sentence and put down a card. The card represents the sentence.
5 The story-teller begins.
6 After two or three sentences, the leader stops the story-teller, points to a sentence card and asks someone to reproduce the sentence. The leader does this after every two to three sentences.
7 Take twenty minutes to tell the story this way. At the end one person tells the whole story.
8 Everybody writes their version of the story. They have another fifteen minutes to do this.

---

2 After a good 30 minutes you go back into the classroom and deal with any problems the students may have with their texts. This is the time for gentle correction and language enrichment.

### NOTE 1

Instead of coloured squares you could use the cuisinaire rods often associated with maths. These rods of different colours and sizes are easy to handle and represent sentences better than cardboard.

### NOTE 2

If you repeat the exercise outlined under *Variation* it's possible to get the students to choose which grammar area they want to work on. (Since the idea of the lesson is to train the learners to learn independently, it's probably not a good idea for the teacher to designate a grammar area.) The above technique is easily adapted to summarising a text, which is part of many exam syllabuses.

### ACKNOWLEDGEMENT

The main exercise above is a version of the 'Islamabad technique' outlined in *A Way and Ways* (p. 139) by Earl Stevick. We learnt the variation from Dick Edelstein.

## 3.1  Achievements

| | |
|---|---|
| GRAMMAR: | *By* + time-phrases |
| | Past perfect |
| LEVEL: | Lower intermediate |
| TIME: | 20 – 30 minutes |
| MATERIALS: | Set of prepared sentences |

THIS ACTIVITY ALSO WORKS WELL WITH: PRESENT PERFECT + *YET, LIKE DOING, LIKE HAVING DONE,* AND MODALS

## Preparation

Think of your achievements in the period of your life that corresponds to the average age of your class. If you are teaching seventeen-year-olds, pick your first seventeen years. Also think of a few of the times when you were slow to achieve. Write sentences about yourself like this (these are real ones about me):

By the age of six I had learnt to read.
I still hadn't learnt to ride a bike by then.
I had got over my fear of water by the time I was eight.
By the time I was nine I had got the hang of riding a bike.
By thirteen I had read a mass of books.
I'd got over my fear of the dark by around ten.

Write ten to twelve sentences using the patterns above. If you are working in a culture that is anti-boasting then pick achievements that do not make you stand out.

Your class will relate well to sentences that tell them something new about you, as much as you feel comfortable telling them. Communication works best when it's for real. What have you to hide? Your students know you intimately whether you give them information or not.

## In class

1 Ask the students to have two different coloured pens ready. Tell them you are going to dictate sentences about yourself. They are to take down the sentences that are also true for them in one colour and the sentences that are not true about them in another colour.
2 Put the students in fours to explain to each other which of your sentences were also true of their lives.

3 Run a quick question-and-answer session round the group, e.g. 'At what age had you learnt to ski/dance/sing/play table tennis etc. by?' 'I'd learnt to ski by seven.'
4 Ask each student to write a couple of fresh sentences about things achieved by a certain date/time and come up and write them on the board or OHP. Wait till the board is full, without correcting what they are putting up. Now point silently at problem sentences and get the students to correct them.

## Variation

You can use the above activity for any area of grammar you want to personalise. You might write sentences about:
- things you haven't got round to doing (present perfect + *yet*)
- things you like having done for you versus things you like doing for yourself
- things you ought to do and feel you can't do (the whole modal area is easily treated within this frame)

### ACKNOWLEDGEMENT

John Morgan, co-author of *Once Upon a Time* told me how he used the above exercise shape to work on the habitual past (*used to*, *would* and *-ed*) + adverbs of frequency.

# 3.2 Typical questions

| | |
|---|---|
| GRAMMAR: | Question formation – varied interrogatives |
| LEVEL: | Beginner to elementary |
| TIME: | 20 – 30 minutes |
| MATERIALS: | None |

## In class

1 Ask the students to draw a quick sketch of a four-year-old they know well. Give them these typical questions such a person may ask, e.g. 'Mummy, does the moon go for a wee-wee?' 'Where did I come from?' Ask each student to write half a dozen questions such a person might ask, writing them in speech bubbles on the drawing. Go round and help with the grammar.

2 Get the students to fill the board with their most interesting four-year-old questions.

Mummy, does the moon go for a wee-wee?

### Variations

This can be used with various question situations. The following examples work well:

– Ask the students to imagine a court room – the prosecution barrister is questioning a defence witness. Tell the student to write a dozen questions the prosecution might ask.

– What kind of questions might a woman going to a foreign country want to ask a woman friend living in this country about the men or the women in the country? And what might a man want to ask a man?

– What kind of questions are you shocked to be asked in an English-speaking country and what questions are you surprised not to be asked?

FEELINGS AND GRAMMAR

## 3.3

# Did you write that?

GRAMMAR: Verbs of liking and disliking + gerund
Past question form with relative pronoun
Reported speech
LEVEL: Elementary to intermediate
TIME: 30 – 45 minutes
MATERIALS: None

## In class

1 Divide the class into groups of about ten or twelve students and appoint a leader for each group.
2 Have everyone write an English word they really like on a slip of paper and have the group leaders collect these.
3 Suggest a selection of verbs of liking and disliking, e.g.: **I don't like, I can't stand, I hate, I loathe, I detest, I like, I really like, I love, I'm crazy about.** Ask students to write secretly, on a slip of paper, one thing that they hate or love doing but that their best mates would be surprised to find that they hated or loved. Ask the group leader to collect in the slips.
4 Have everyone write a list on a blank sheet of paper of the names of all the classmates in their sub-group.
5 Ask the group leader to read out the favourite word lists. Tell the students to write each favourite word next to the name of the student who they guess wrote it. The group leaders then dictate the like/dislike sentences and the students again write them next to the supposed author.
6 Give the class the question:
**Did you write that your favourite word was ...?**
Have a round of questions in each group simultaneously. Each student can ask only one question to any other student in the group. The students keep track of what has been discovered on their sheets. There may need to be two or three rounds.
7 Now give the structures:
**Was it you who wrote you hated/loved ...*ing*?** or
**Is it you who wrote you loved/hated ...*ing*?**
Proceed as in step 6.

NOTE
Although there is a lot of repetition and drill-like practice of structure in this exercise, the main purpose is to get people to listen to each other.

## 3.4  Who wrote what about me?

| | |
|---|---|
| GRAMMAR: | Verbs that take the gerund |
| LEVEL: | Lower to upper intermediate |
| TIME: | 30 – 40 minutes |
| MATERIALS: | One **Gerund sheet** per student |

THIS ACTIVITY CAN BE ADAPTED FOR USE WITH OTHER GRAMMATICAL STRUCTURES

### In class

1  Give out a **Gerund sheet** to each person in the class. Ask each student to complete the sentences thinking about different classmates and using a gerund construction after the verb, e.g. Juan resents having to wash his hair or Ludwiga enjoys teasing people.
Each sentence should mention a different classmate. Tell the students to put their own names at the top of the sheet. Go round helping and correcting as the students write.
2  Take in all the completed sheets and then hand them out again, making sure nobody gets their own.
3  The students mill round the room in search of all the sentences people have written about them or people they are interested in. They have a chance to say whether other people's projections about them are true or not.

### Variation

You can easily use this exercise frame for other grammar patterns. Suppose you are teaching a lower intermediate class a lesson on adjective order, you might ask them to write sentences with two adjectives about their classmates, e.g. 'Abder is a 21-year-old, friendly Palestinian.' Oops … 'a friendly, 21-year-old Palestinian.'

ACKNOWLEDGEMENT

Nicky Burbidge, co-author of *Letters*, did this exercise a different way from above. She wrote gerund sentences about her students who had to mill round the classroom checking out which of her statements were true.
Our version is an adaptation of Nicky's exercise. We agree with Sheelagh Deller in her book *Lessons from the Learners* that lots of things teachers do can be done better by the students themselves.

FEELINGS AND GRAMMAR

## GERUND SHEET

*Write about your classmates using the verbs below – they are given in the infinitive form – you can use any tense. After each verb you need a gerund. You may decide to write more than one sentence about a particular classmate.*

My name: .......................................................

(to enjoy) ........................................................................

(to risk) ........................................................................

(to practise) ........................................................................

(to appreciate) ........................................................................

(can't help) ........................................................................

(to resent) ........................................................................

(to not mind) ........................................................................

(to consider) ........................................................................

(can't resist) ........................................................................

(to avoid) ........................................................................

(can/can't imagine) ........................................................................

(to detest) ........................................................................

(to dislike) ........................................................................

(to often feel like) ........................................................................

(to mind) ........................................................................

(to give up) ........................................................................

(to put off) ........................................................................

(can't face) ........................................................................

(to miss) ........................................................................

(to finish) ........................................................................

(to put off / postpone) ........................................................................

(to deny) ........................................................................

WHO WROTE WHAT ABOUT ME?

# 3.5 In-groups and out-groups

| | |
|---|---|
| GRAMMAR: | Varied interrogatives |
| LEVEL: | Elementary to advanced |
| TIME: | 20 – 40 minutes |
| MATERIALS: | None |

YOU CAN ADAPT THIS ACTIVITY TO MANY DIFFERENT GRAMMATICAL STRUCTURES

## In class

1 Explain that you are going to divide the class into male and female sub-groups. (See below for other groupings if your class is all one sex.) Tell them you want them to pair off within their groups and write twelve to fifteen questions to ask members of the other group about belonging to the sex group they do. If possible, ask either the females or the males to go to another room or space. If you can't do this, ask the pairs to work in male and female blocks in different parts of your classroom.

2 Ask the female pairs to work with the males, forming groups of four. They fire the questions they have written at the other pair.

## Variation 1

You can use this exercise productively with all sorts of groups, e.g.:
    smokers versus non-smokers
    believers versus non-believers
    meat-eaters versus vegetarians
    supporters of one team versus supporters of another
    dreamers in colour versus dreamers in black and white
    left-handers and ambidextrous people versus right-handers
    children of non-divorced families versus children of divorced families
(Some of the above group belongings are very first-worldish – you will know the relevant groupings to choose for your students.)

## Variation 2

Ask the people in group A to go away in their pairs and come up with questions they guess people from group B will want to ask them. When the pairs from groups A and B come together they exchange lists of questions, so that the group A people end up answering the questions they have written themselves, put to them by group B people.

## Grammar variations

You can use this exercise with many different structures:
- Ask the students to make grammatically negative sentences about the other group.
- Ask the students to make hypothetical statements about the other group, e.g. *Maybe they sometimes ... / I wonder if they ... / could be that they ...*

ACKNOWLEDGEMENT

The idea for this exercise came in the course of a workshop on countering racism held in Weimar for VHS teachers, organised by Heinz Reiske from Hessen and Friedrich Hutener from Thueringen.

IN-GROUPS AND OUT-GROUPS

# 3.6

# Verbs for extroverts

GRAMMAR: Verbs followed by *with* (reciprocal verbs)
LEVEL: Intermediate to advanced
TIME: 20 – 30 minutes
MATERIALS: One copy of **The questionnaire** per student

## Preparation

Think of an extrovert, pushy person you know well. Be ready to draw a picture of them on the board.

## In class

1 Draw a picture on the board of the pushy person you have decided on. Tell the group two or three things about them.
2 Give out **The questionnaire** so the students can ask you about your person (you may have to explain some of the verbs). Give full, reflective answers. At the end of the questioning phase point out that all but one of the verbs in the questionnaire are followed by *with*.
3 Ask each student to draw a picture of someone they know who is extrovert and pushy. Tell them the worse the drawing is, the better it is for the exercise!
4 Pair the students. Person A administers the questionnaire to person B. Then they do it the other way round.

FEELINGS AND GRAMMAR

## THE QUESTIONNAIRE

What did you say the person's name is?

Who does ............. (*name*) mostly mix with?

Who does ............. quarrel with?

Who does he or she compete with?

Who does he or she avoid mixing with?

Who does ............. talk with most? What about, mostly?

Who clashes with them most? Over what?

Who do they usually consult with? On what?

Who do they often agree with? About what?

What problems does ............. have to contend with at home, at work?

© Cambridge University Press 1995

## GRAMMAR NOTE

The *Collins COBUILD English Grammar*, edited by John Sinclair, gives a useful list of reciprocal verbs.

## 3.7

# *To* versus *-ing*

GRAMMAR:  Verbs + *-ing* / verbs + infinitive with *to*
LEVEL:    Upper intermediate to advanced
TIME:     3 minutes in first class / 20 – 30 minutes in second class
MATERIALS: One copy of the *To versus -ing* sheet per student

## In class

1  At the end of the *first lesson* give out the **To versus -ing** sheet and ask the students to complete it for homework.
2  In the *second lesson* do a speedy check to see that most people got the right verb forms.
3  Pair the students and ask them to tell each other some of the stories behind their sentences. Encourage questions. While this is going on, check the verb forms over people's shoulders.

---

### *TO* VERSUS *-ING*

*On a separate sheet complete these sentence stems meaningfully, talking about your own experience. Use either the 'gerund' or the 'infinitive', as grammatically appropriate. Do **not** use nouns.*

I'll never forget … (describe a vivid event)
I'm afraid I often postpone …
When I'm not feeling confident, I dread …
As a child I would often pretend …
I have always meant … (something you haven't done)
I absolutely loathe …
I never get round to …
As a kid I used to resent …
When I get home from school or work I often fancy …
Am I ambitious? Well, I aim …
I'm afraid I don't dare … (something you are scared to do)
I try to keep my promises. I remember once I promised …
I really can't afford …

© Cambridge University Press 1995

---

FEELINGS AND GRAMMAR

## 3.8  Telling people what they feel

GRAMMAR: Imperative, imperative with *don't*, *stop* + gerund, *mind you …*, *never mind about -ing*

LEVEL: Intermediate to advanced

TIME: 40 – 50 minutes

MATERIALS: One copy of **Sensible advice** per student

## In class

1  Give out **Sensible advice** and ask students to underline all the sentences they think make this a *female* text and, using a different colour, all the sentences that make this a *male* text. (There are no absolute linguistic indicators – what people are working on is their own perception of maternal or paternal behaviour. The writer was a man but don't tell the students yet.)

2  In threes they compare the sentences they have underlined.

3  Ask them to copy out all the sentences from the text that they have heard in their own families or other people's.

4  They compare the sentences they have copied out (in threes).

5  Ask them to write a list of ten to twelve 'parental' utterances they would or do avoid using with their own children.

## SENSIBLE ADVICE

Stop loafing about you two. Hey! You're too old to be doing that! Don't make faces. Don't point. Put that tongue back in right this minute. Don't run on the edge of the pond. A policeman will come and take you away. Watch it, you'll put someone's eye out with that thing.

Come away from that dog. It's a disgusting dog. Don't let it near your face. You're getting sunburnt. You are, you're getting red. You're cold, yes you are, you're shivering. And you're overtired. Don't contradict me, you're overtired! You went to bed too late last night, but would you listen? You'll all be in bed by eight o'clock tonight. Don't show your temper to me. Don't care was made to care. Tie your laces or you'll fall over them and cut your head open.

Your face is far too red. Go and sit in the room. In fact let's all go and sit in the room. Come on, who wants to get a video and we'll all go and sit in the room. Yes, all right, Burger Kings and a video and we'll watch a … stop that you two!

No, you can't go back in the water, we're going to watch a video in the room. Never mind about your sunblock. No, the waterpark's closed. Well, it is, smartie pants, actually for your information. Closed every Sunday morning for routine maintenance. So stop running in the aisles. Of course you can't have that video, are you mad? A policeman will come and take you away. Yes he will. I'll ring them up myself and have you arrested. Come away from there. Come out of there. Put that down, do you want to put someone's eye out? Don't do that with your T-shirt. Mind your feet. Get out of my way. No, you can't have any money. Don't you threaten me, young lady, Social Services* will not be interested. Don't! You'll put somebody's eye out with that thing.

Use your napkins. Sit up properly. Don't do that with your T-shirt. You're much too burnt. Leave that alone, it's my drink. No, you can't have any beer. Take your feet off the table. Stop throwing that ball around. If you splash that water, you'll clean it all up. You've had a lovely day, don't spoil it now. No. Stop it. Don't.

How much longer did you say your holidays were?

(From *The Independent*)

## NOTE

For some students this exercise may raise strong feelings – watch for signs of distress in steps 3–5.

* In the 90s there were several scandals in the UK with Social Services overstepping their legal right to interfere in family life.

FEELINGS AND GRAMMAR

# 3.9

# Reported advice

GRAMMAR: Modals and modals reported
LEVEL: Elementary to intermediate
TIME: 15 – 20 minutes
MATERIALS: None

## In class

1 Divide your class into two groups: 'problem people' and 'advice givers'.
2 Ask the 'problem people' to each think up a minor problem they have and are willing to talk about.
3 Arm the 'advice givers' with these suggestion forms:

You *could* ...        You *should* ...        You *might as well* ...
You *might* ...        You *ought to* ...      You *might try ...ing* ...

4 Get the class moving round the room. Tell each 'problem person' to pair off with an 'advice giver'. The 'problem person' explains her problem and the other person gives two bits of advice using the grammar suggested. Each 'problem person' now moves on to another 'advice giver'. The 'problem people' get advice from five or six 'advice givers'.
5 Call the class back into plenary. Ask some of the 'problem people' to state their problem and report to the whole group on the best and the worst piece of advice they were offered, naming the advice giver, e.g. 'Juan was telling me I should give her up.' 'Concepción suggested I ought to get a girlfriend of hers to talk to her for me.'

### Variation

If you have a classroom with space that allows it, form the students into two concentric circles, the outer one facing in and the inner one facing out. All the inner circle students are 'advice givers' and all the outer circle students are 'problem people'. After each round, the outer circle people move round three places. This is much more cohesive than the above.

ACKNOWLEDGEMENT
We learnt this exercise from Grethe Hooper Hanson during a workshop at The Cambridge Academy.

## 3.10 Impersonating members of a set

| | |
|---|---|
| GRAMMAR: | Present and past simple – active and passive |
| LEVEL: | Elementary to intermediate |
| TIME: | 20 – 30 minutes |
| MATERIALS: | None |

### In class

1 Ask people to brainstorm all the things they can think of that give off light.
2 Choose one of these yourself and become the thing chosen. Describe yourself in around five to six sentences, e.g.:

I am a candle.
I start very big and end up as nothing.
My head is lit and I produce a flame.
I burn down slowly.
In some countries I am put on a Christmas tree.
I am old-fashioned and very fashionable.

3 Ask a couple of other students to choose other light sources and do the same as you have just done. Help them with language. They use the first person, e.g. 'I am a light bulb – I was invented by Edison …'
4 Group the students in sixes. Give them a new category to choose an item from to impersonate, e.g. things you write with. Ask them to work silently, writing five or six first-person sentences in role, such as a biro, quill pen or PC keyboard. Go round and help, especially with vocabulary and the formation of the present simple passive (when this help is needed).
5 In their groups the students read out their sentences.
6 Ask each group to choose their six most interesting sentences. These are then read out to the whole group.

FEELINGS AND GRAMMAR

## Variation

The exercise is sometimes more exciting if done with fairly abstract sets, e.g. numbers between 50 and 149, musical notes, distances, weights.
The abstract nature of the set makes people concretise interestingly, e.g.:

I am a kilometre.
My son is a metre and my baby is a centimetre.
On the motorway I am driven in 30 seconds. (*120 kms. per hour*)

We have also used these sets: types of stone / countries / items of clothing (e.g. socks, skirts, jackets) / times of day / smells / family roles (e.g. son, mother etc.) / types of weather.

### RATIONALE

The sentences students produce in this exercise are not repeat runs of things they have already thought and said in mother tongue. New standpoints, new thoughts, new language. The English is fresh because the thought is.

### ACKNOWLEDGEMENT

One grey, autumn Sunday morning Bruno Rinvolucri came up with this thought frame. He was seven and three-quarters at the time. He first came up with the abstract frames, e.g. numbers and letters of the alphabet.

# Choosing the passive

| | |
|---|---|
| GRAMMAR: | Past simple passive *versus* past simple active |
| LEVEL: | Intermediate |
| TIME: | 40 – 50 minutes |
| MATERIALS: | One copy of the **Passive / active list** per student |

## In class

1  To set the mood, describe a piece of furniture you liked as a child, where it was in the house and why you liked it, what you did with it etc.
2  Ask the students to do the same in twos or threes.
3  Give out the **Passive / active list** and ask them to work individually. In each pair of sentences they underline the one that fits their personal story best. Ask them to feel free to change any verbs that don't fit, e.g. *loved* might become *ignored*. One or two of the sentences may not connect with them at all – tell them to omit these.

---

### PASSIVE / ACTIVE LIST

| | |
|---|---|
| I was born. | I pushed out of my mother's womb. |
| I was taught to yawn. | I gave my first yawn. |
| I was shown how to crawl. | I crawled all over the floor. |
| I was loved by my Mum. | I loved my Mum. |
| I was toilet-trained. | I used a potty. |
| I was told to fight my brother/sister. | I fought with my brother/sister. |
| I was taken to nursery school. | I went to nursery school. |
| I was befriended by other kids. | I made friends with other kids. |
| I was loved by my Dad. | I loved my Dad. |
| I was sent to 'big school'. | I went to 'big school'. |
| I was taught to read. | I learnt how to read. |
| I was taught how to write. | I got myself writing. |
| I was made to feel happy at school. | I felt happy at school. |
| I was given homework. | I did school things at home. |
| I was sometimes punished. | I sometimes provoked them into punishing me. |
| I was fed at school. | I ate at school. |

© Cambridge University Press 1995

---

4 Group the students in fours to explain their choices.
5 Now ask students to think about the recent past and to bring to mind six to eight things that have happened to them. They work on their own and write a passive and active version of each event, e.g. 'I decided to go to Paris' *versus* 'I was sent to Paris'. They underline the one that best suits the situation. You go round and help with language.
6 Group them in fours to share their sentences and reasons for choice of voice.

# 3.12    A sprinkling of people

GRAMMAR: Collective nouns
LEVEL: Upper intermediate to advanced
TIME: 50 – 60 minutes
MATERIALS: One copy of the **Collective phrase questionnaire** per student

## In class

1 Tell the students you are going to dictate a list of phrases to them. Ask them to estimate and write down the number of individuals they would expect to find in each collective, e.g. 'a herd of elephants: 10–30'.
A clump of trees / a party of tourists / a gang of terrorists / a unit of freedom fighters / a fleet of ships / a spate of rumours / a troop of monkeys / a gaggle of geese / a squadron of fighter planes / a clutch of eggs / a sea of faces / a pride of lions / a hail of bullets / a pack of wolves / a litter of kittens / a school of dolphins / a flight of steps.

2 Write up the words you reckon may have been misspelt. The students check the meanings with you.

3 Get estimates from round the class of the numbers in typical groups e.g. 'a clump of trees is a lot less than a little wood'.

4 Ask them to identify the five phrases that are *least* easy to translate into their mother tongue (a language like Greek has far fewer highly specific collective nouns than English). They compare phrases.

5 Explain that in English you sometimes have a choice of collective nouns. Tell them you will read out pairs of phrases – they are to take down the one they prefer in each pair. Read each pair of phrases twice:

| | |
|---|---|
| a flock of birds | a flight of birds |
| a swarm of insects | a colony of insects |
| a herd of goats | a flock of goats |
| a troupe of actors | a company of actors |
| a wad of banknotes | a roll of banknotes |
| a pack of cards | a deck of cards |
| a team of experts | a panel of experts |
| a bunch of grapes | a cluster of grapes |
| a sheaf of papers | a bundle of papers |
| a crowd of reporters | a gaggle of reporters |
| a gang of thieves | a pack of thieves |

FEELINGS AND GRAMMAR

6 Write up any words they are unsure how to spell, e.g. 'troupe' rather than 'troop'.
7 Group them in threes to explain their choices of phrase.
8 Now pair the students and give out the **Collective phrase questionnaire** below. Ask the students to work through it, each answering each of the questions.

---

## COLLECTIVE PHRASE QUESTIONNAIRE

- Have you ever been in a party of tourists? How many of you were there?
- Can you think of a clump of trees near your house? Roughly how many trees?
- Have you ever seen a shoal of fish? Where? What time of day was it?
- What do you call a big group of bees on the wing? When did you last see a swarm of bees?
- What do you feel on seeing a litter of new-born puppies?
- When did you last carry round a wad of banknotes? Do you often do this? How do you feel if it is a really thick roll?
- Have you ever baked a cake? Have you ever baked a batch of cakes or tarts?
- I bet you have a bunch of keys in your bag/pocket. How many in the bunch?
- Is there a flight of steps near your home? How long would it / does it take you to get up them? How many steps are there, approximately?
- How many cards are there in a deck of cards? Are there any special cards in your country with a different number in the pack?
- When did you last give someone a bouquet of flowers? Or receive a bunch of flowers?
- What would you mean if you said that most of the audience in the theatre were Japanese but that there was also a sprinkling of French?

© Cambridge University Press 1995

---

## ACKNOWLEDGEMENT

*Collins COBUILD English Usage*, p. 280 provided the information this exercise is built on.

## 3.13

# Us lot

GRAMMAR: Quantifiers
LEVEL: Elementary to intermediate
TIME: 20 – 30 minutes
MATERIALS: None

## In class

1 Put these quantifiers up on the board:

| | |
|---|---|
| *loads and loads* of students | *several* students |
| *a lot of* students | *not many* students |
| *quite a few* students | *few* students |
| *not all* students | *one or two* students |
| *a good few* students | *a few good* students |
| *some* students | *too many* students |

Ask each student to write twelve sentences using each quantifier once and making statements about the school, e.g. 'Some students have brothers and sisters here.' 'Not many students have foreign parents.'

2 Put the students in groups of four or five and ask them to compare their statements.

## Variation

Ask students to do the same exercise but to pick another group they belong to, not the school, e.g.:

their extended family
their mosque or church or temple
a sporting group they belong to
a political party
their class (rather than the whole school)

### ACKNOWLEDGEMENT

Clare Anderson at the Cambridge Eurocentre had students complete quantifier stems like those above to get them to find their way around the school's self-study centre, e.g. 'Not many students are asleep.' 'There are very few Arabic–English dictionaries' etc.

FEELINGS AND GRAMMAR

# Lack

| | |
|---|---|
| GRAMMAR: | Noun to adjective transformation adding *less* |
| LEVEL: | Upper intermediate to advanced |
| TIME: | 40 – 50 minutes |
| MATERIALS: | One copy per pair of the **Semantic questionnaire** |
| | One copy per pair of the **Semantic questionnaire key** |
| | One copy per pair of the **Personal questionnaires** |

## In class

1 Brainstorm the idea of *lack*. Get the students to fill the board with ideas connected with *lack*, e.g. dearth, drought, short of etc.
2 Pair the students and give out the **Semantic questionnaire**, one to each pair. Ask them to work through this, using a dictionary where necessary.
3 Give out the **Semantic questionnaire key** and cope with things the students bring up.
4 Pair the students. Give out one of the **Personal questionnaires** to person A in each pair and the other to person B. Tell the students to ask their questions.

See following pages for questionnaires. ▶

## SEMANTIC QUESTIONNAIRE

1 Can you think of a synonym for **anonymous** that ends in **less**?

2 Suppose you are astonished and dumbfounded by something – you simply can't open your mouth – you are left ............**less**.

3 You go running and you pant a lot – one could describe you as being ............**less** or **out** ............ .

4 Can you find a word ending in **less** to describe a military commander who kills all his prisoners?

5 Have you ever run a half marathon? After an hour's running the way ahead can seem ............**less**.

6 How about a ............**less** word for unnecessary?

7 You can talk about a man of **limitless** means (pots of money) but can you talk about a man of **limitful** means?

8 A dress that is too large and doesn't fit you can be described as ............**less**.

9 What's the opposite of a sensible idea?

10 Give a synonym for 'still' in the sentence 'He stood absolutely still'.

11 If a person does something unkind and rough to you, you can accuse them of being ............**less**.

12 Do you understand this phrase: 'umpteen overland as tomorrowified'? You could describe the phrase as ............**less**.

13 To say a 'dead corpse' sounds odd but you can say 'a ............**less** corpse'.

14 What is the opposite of 'kind', ending in **less**? (use a part of the body)

15 If something is **harmless**, does it mean no harm will come to it?

16 Do you think 'pregnant' is the opposite of **childless**?

17 If you have hyper-inflation, the currency becomes ............**less**. What's the opposite adjective?

18 She has been a teacher, a plumber and has had a huge number of other jobs too. She has had ............**less** jobs.

19 Is there any group of **landless** people in your country? Who?

20 Saving pennies for the fun of it, if you yourself are well-off, is pretty ............**less**.

FEELINGS AND GRAMMAR

## SEMANTIC QUESTIONNAIRE KEY

1 nameless (or faceless) 2 speechless (*'wordless' does not fit as well here*) 3 breathless or out-of-breath 4 merciless or ruthless (*'heartless' is too weak*) 5 endless 6 needless 7 no 8 shapeless 9 senseless 10 motionless 11 thoughtless or heartless (*'thoughtless' implies they are unaware*) 12 meaningless 13 lifeless 14 heartless 15 no 16 no, because a childless woman is not necessarily a barren woman 17 worthless; strong 18 countless 19 (*student's own answer*) 20 pointless



## PERSONAL QUESTIONNAIRE A

### *Student A (to student B)*

1 When was the last time you felt relatively helpless? Tell me about it. What happened then?
2 When did someone in authority last set you a pointless task? What was it? How did you react?
3 Waiting can seem endless. Does it ever happen to you?
4 Have you ever read a book you feel is timeless? Why does it have this quality of timelessness for you?
5 Are your thought processes ever shapeless and all over the place? What do you do about it?
6 When were you last left speechless with delight?
7 Have you ever been in a situation where you felt powerless? Say more.

## PERSONAL QUESTIONNAIRE B

*Student B (to student A)*

1 Do you know of anyone who is really careless on the road? What sort of mistakes do they make?
2 Can you remember the last time you felt really breathless? Have you ever felt out-of-breath in a dream?
3 In what situations do you get restless? Is there a lot of restlessness in your family?
4 Do you know of anybody whose behaviour often strikes you as thoughtless? What sorts of things do they do?
5 What has been your most senseless purchase this year? How come you bought it?
6 Who is the most hopeless person you know? What sort of things do they get up to?



### NOTE

The *Collins COBUILD English Grammar*, edited by John Sinclair, suggests that English has a number of 'productive features' that allow you to safely create new bits of language. Adding *less* to a noun is one of these.

### ACKNOWLEDGEMENT

The *less* compounds chosen come from the list given in the *Collins COBUILD English Grammar*, edited by John Sinclair.
The **Semantic questionnaire** draws on the thinking of Roger Bowers et al. in *Speaking of English*.

## 3.15 Haves and have-nots

GRAMMAR: Multiple uses of the verb *have*
LEVEL: Intermediate to advanced
TIME: 40 – 50 minutes
MATERIALS: **Dictation sentences** (for your use only)
Photocopies of **Haves and have-nots** worksheet (optional)

## In class

1 Give out a copy of **Haves and have-nots** worksheet to each student. Alternatively, you could get the students to make the worksheet: Tell them to turn their pages longways and rule four columns with the following headings:
   (1) **I smell / I taste**   (2) **I hear**   (3) **I see**   (4) **I feel through my body**

2 Tell the students you are going to dictate short sentences to them. Ask them to experience these as situations. If they first *hear* the situation they write it in column two. If they first *feel* the situation they write it in column four etc. Many people will see, hear and feel many of the situations. The choice of column is governed by which of these things they actually do *first* – what pops up first from the unconscious.

3 Dictate each sentence/phrase twice, leaving time for students to conjure up the situations.

4 Put the students in threes and ask them to compare where they put the sentences. Ask them to share some of the situations they smelled, heard, saw or felt.

5 Ask them to go back over the sentences and decide which, when translated into their mother tongue, would not have the equivalent of the verb *to have* in them. (In Italian you *make* a dream and in both Greek and Japanese you *see* a dream.)

### DICTATION SENTENCES

I have a headache.
I went to hospital and had a baby.
I have it in me to do great things.
I had a good breakfast.
She had it off with him.
Children love to have stories read to them.
She had some money stolen.

I had a dream last night.
I had my head down.
I had a small operation on my nose.
He hates him – he really has it in for him.
The police had me up for speeding.
We had the grass cut.
I have two very good friends.
Just listen to that radio – it's had it.

---

## HAVES AND HAVE-NOTS

*I smell / I taste*

................................................

................................................

................................................

................................................

................................................

................................................

................................................

................................................

*I hear*

................................................

................................................

................................................

................................................

................................................

................................................

................................................

................................................

*I see*

................................................

................................................

................................................

................................................

................................................

................................................

................................................

................................................

*I feel through my body*

................................................

................................................

................................................

................................................

................................................

................................................

................................................

................................................

ACKNOWLEDGEMENT

We learnt the sensory categorisation from Neuro-Linguistic Programming (NLP) and there is another similar exercise from this 'feeder field' in *Dictation* by Paul Davis and Mario Rinvolucri.

FEELINGS AND GRAMMAR

## 3.16　Picture the past

GRAMMAR: Past simple, past perfect, future in the past
LEVEL: Lower intermediate
TIME: 20 – 40 minutes
MATERIALS: None

## In class

1　Ask three students to come out and help you demonstrate the exercise. Draw a picture on the board of something interesting you have done. Do not speak about it. Student A then writes a past simple sentence about it. Student B writes about what had already happened before the picture action and student C about something that was going to happen, using the appropriate grammar.

2　Put the students in fours. Each draws a picture of a real past action of theirs. They pass their picture silently to a neighbour in the foursome who adds a past tense sentence. Pass the picture again and each adds a past perfect sentence. They pass again and each adds a *was going to* sentence. All this is done in silence with you going round helping and correcting.

3　In their fours, they compare the pictures and sentences. The sentences frequently reinterpret the pictures in an amusing way.

ACKNOWLEDGEMENT

We learnt this exercise from Christine Frank during a technical evening at the Pilgrims Summer Institute in 1993.

85

## 3.17    Passive verbs

GRAMMAR: Transitive verbs usually found in the passive
LEVEL: Advanced
TIME: Homework and 30 – 40 minutes in class
MATERIALS: One copy of **Passivity A questionnaire** and **Passivity B questionnaire** for each member of your class

## In first class

Give half the group copies of the **Passivity A questionnaire** and the other half copies of the **Passivity B questionnaire**. For homework ask the students to look up all words that are unfamiliar and to complete their questionnaires.

## In second class

Pair the students. Student A fires her questions at student B who answers them. They then work the other way round. Give out the remaining questionnaires so each student has **Passivity A questionnaire** and **Passivity B questionnaire**. Give help where needed with the sentences the students have created.

ACKNOWLEDGEMENT
The extremely useful list of transitive verbs normally found in the passive (from the *Collins COBUILD English Grammar*, edited by John Sinclair) led us to devise this exercise.

FEELINGS AND GRAMMAR

## PASSIVITY A QUESTIONNAIRE

*Read the questions below and check out words you don't know well. In the spaces we have left, frame questions of your own using the passive verbs provided. These verbs are most commonly used in the passive voice.*

1 Have you ever been stranded late at night with no transport and had to find some way of getting home? Describe what happened.

2 Is there any tradition in your family of anybody having ever been shipwrecked? Do you know of anybody outside your family who has? Has anyone you know ever been involved in a plane crash or near-miss situation?

3 Do you know anyone who has been paralysed? Tell me something about them, please, about how they got paralysed and about how they cope.

4 Have you ever felt your life dwarfed by greater events happening around you? If yes, say more.

5 To be hospitalised (*please write a question to put to a classmate using this verb*)

   .....................................................................................................................

6 To be deafened .................................................................................................

   .....................................................................................................................

7 To be born ........................................................................................................

   .....................................................................................................................

8 Can you think of a time when you were alleged to have done something unpleasant, which in fact you did not do? Can you outline the situation and the outcome?

9 Can you think of a case in which two people fell out badly, but were subsequently reconciled to each other? What exactly happened?

10 Are you the kind of person that gets mesmerised by a book, an event or another person? Do you know anyone who gets mesmerised in this way?

11 Have you ever noticed a person being unjustly pilloried for actions or opinions that were not theirs?

12 When were you last taken aback by someone's reaction to something you did or said?

13 To be baffled by ...............................................................................................

   .....................................................................................................................

14 To be buried .....................................................................................................

   .....................................................................................................................

PASSIVE VERBS

## PASSIVITY B QUESTIONNAIRE

*Read the questions below and check out any words you don't know well. In the spaces we have left, frame questions of your own using the passive verbs provided. These verbs are most commonly used in the passive voice.*

1  Do you know anyone whose house has been gutted by fire? If so, say more.
2  On your way somewhere you must sometimes have been misdirected – can you recall amusing instances?
3  In what ways do you think you were conditioned by being at school? Give three examples of such conditioning.
4  To be fined (*please write a question using this verb to be put to a classmate*)

   ......................................................................................................................................

5  To be shortlisted for a job or scholarship ...................................................................

   ......................................................................................................................................

6  Can you think of times when you have been literally swamped by having far too many things to do?
7  Tell me three things you are disconcerted by. Do you think you are right to be disconcerted this way?
8  Have you ever been inundated with mail? If so, say more, and if not, do you know of anybody else who has?
9  Can you bring to mind a film or book character who is emotionally wiped out by some event? Describe the scene.
10  Are there any public or family events that you know of that are still shrouded in mystery?
11  To be reunited with ...............................................................................................

   ......................................................................................................................................

12  To be wounded (physically or emotionally) ............................................................

   ......................................................................................................................................

13  To be injured .........................................................................................................

   ......................................................................................................................................

14  Have you ever been deemed by people in your circle to have been really successful at something? Example please.

© Cambridge University Press 1995

**4.1**

# Whose am I?

| | |
|---|---|
| GRAMMAR: | 's genitive + animate + human |
| LEVEL: | Beginner |
| TIME: | 15 – 20 minutes |
| MATERIALS: | None |

## In class

1 Revise the words below which the students already know and teach the others.

| | | | | |
|---|---|---|---|---|
| father | uncle | niece | flatmate | boss |
| mother | aunt | wife | classmate | colleague |
| son | sister | husband | friend | enemy |
| daughter | brother | twin | boyfriend | ex-friend |
| grandson | nephew | cousin | girfriend | ex-husband etc. |

2 Explain to the students you are going to tell them about people close to you. Ask one person to come out and sit with you in front of the group as your special listener. You speak for a minute (time yourself).
  If I were teaching your class I might start this way: 'I'm Giuseppe's son and Sophie's husband. I'm Bernie's brother and Paul's friend and colleague. I'm not a cousin.'
  When you have finished your minute, the listener has to repeat back to you what you said as best they can. You may have to prompt them here and there.

3 Tell the class to pair off and do the exercise you have just demonstrated. Stress the importance of the listener really listening (no note taking). You time the groups. Each person in the pair has a turn at speaking.

4 Finish the exercise with each student drawing a diagram of the people their neighbour 'belongs to', e.g.:

Giuseppe's son

↑

Paul's friend ⟵—— MARIO ——⟶ Bernie's brother

↓

Sophie's husband

**89**

# 4.2  No backshift

| | |
|---|---|
| GRAMMAR: | Reported speech without backshift after past reporting verb |
| LEVEL: | Elementary to lower intermediate |
| TIME: | 15 – 20 minutes |
| MATERIAL: | None |

## In class

1  Pair the students. Ask one person in each pair to prepare to speak for two minutes about a pleasurable future event. Give them a minute to prepare.
2  Ask the listener in each pair to prepare to give their whole attention to the speaker. They are not to take notes. Ask the speaker in each pair to get going. You time two minutes.
3  Pair the pairs. The two listeners now report on what they heard using this kind of form:

She **was telling** me *she's going* to Thailand for her holiday and she **added** that she*'ll be going* by plane.

The speakers have the right to fill in things the listeners have left out, but only after the listeners have finished speaking.
4  The students go back into their original pairs and repeat the above steps, but this time with the other one as speaker, so everybody has been able to share their future event thoughts.

### Variation

A starts a conversation with B and before B can say what she wants, she has to report to A on what A has just said. B then says what she wants to say and so on – a radical and very interesting break in normal thought and discourse patterns.

### GRAMMAR NOTE

In the spoken and informal written language you frequently find that the clause following a past simple or continuous tense reporting verb does not backshift. Perhaps it is reasonable to get students reporting in English without backshift before introducing them to this succulent area of grammar! It's worth pointing out when introducing backshift that the form presented above is used in informal situations and for immediacy.

LISTENING TO PEOPLE

# 4.3

# Incomparable

GRAMMAR: Comparative structures
LEVEL: Elementary
TIME: 15 – 20 minutes
MATERIALS: None

## In class

1 Tell the students a bit about yourself by comparing yourself to some people you know:

I'm *more ... than* my husband.
I'm *not as ... as* my eldest boy.
I reckon my uncle is *... than* me.

Write six or seven of these sentences up on the board as a grammar pattern input.

2 Tell the students to work in threes. Two of the three listen very closely while the third compares herself to people she knows. The speakers speak without interruption for 90 seconds and you time them.

3 The two listeners in each group feedback to the speaker exactly what they heard. If they miss things the speaker will want to prompt them.

4 Repeat steps 2 and 3 so that everybody in the group has had a go at producing a comparative self-portrait.

# Round the circle

| | |
|---|---|
| GRAMMAR: | Prepositions of movement |
| LEVEL: | Beginner to elementary |
| TIME: | 10 – 20 minutes |
| MATERIALS: | Soft ball or ball of newspaper |

## In class

1 The whole group stands in a big circle (among fixed benches if necessary). Throw the ball and say your name. If people already know all the names turn it into a spelling exercise: P-A-U-L.
2 Tell the students to throw the ball and say their name and the name of the person being thrown to, e.g. 'From Paul to Ahmed'. As he catches the ball Ahmed says: 'From Paul to me'.
3 In successive rounds try these prepositional patterns:
   a) From A to B *for* X (On catching the ball, B says: 'From A to me for X'. On catching the ball, X says: 'From A to B for me'.)
   b) From A to B *via* X
   c) From A to B *behind X's back*
   d) From A to B *across the floor* (rolling the ball)
   e) From A to B *round the circle* (handing the ball from person to person)
   f) From A to B *clockwise/anti-clockwise round the circle*
   g) From A to B *over X's head*

ACKNOWLEDGEMENT

We learnt this extension of the name-learning, ball-tossing game in the warm-up phase of the psychodrama session led by Ari Bedaines.

From Mark to Ahmed.

LISTENING TO PEOPLE

## 4.5  Eyes shut

GRAMMAR: Present perfect
LEVEL: Elementary to intermediate
TIME: 15 – 25 minutes
MATERIALS: None

THIS CAN BE ADAPTED TO
PRACTISE VIRTUALLY ANY
GRAMMATICAL STRUCTURE

## In class

1 Put a selection of irregular verbs up on the board, e.g.:

| buy | bought | **bought** |
| begin | began | **begun** |
| give | gave | **given** |
| lend | lent | **lent** |
| lose | lost | **lost** |
| see | saw | **seen** |
| sell | sold | **sold** |

Make sure the meanings of the verbs are clear to everybody.

2 Group the students in seated circles of about ten. Explain that they are
going to play a concentration game, with eyes shut. The first student will
make a present perfect sentence about herself, using one of the verbs
given or another of her choice, e.g. 'I've sold my bike'. These sentences
may be either *true* or *false*. Everybody shuts their eyes. The student to
her right then repeats her sentence, in the first person and adds her own,
e.g. 'I've sold my bike, I've begun trampolining'. Student 3, going round
the circle, repeats the first two sentences and adds hers etc.

3 Tell the students to have a good look round their circles before they shut
their eyes. Get the game going. (Some groups manage to go round the
circle more than once, so there are 15, 20, 25 present perfect sentences
being remembered.)

4 Allow the students time to guess which sentences were *true*.

### RATIONALE

Blind exercises are very useful in language learning for drawing people who
may not be primarily auditory into the world of sound. They also allow
auditorily excellent students some of the 'lime-sound' (limelight).

### ACKNOWLEDGEMENT

We learnt this Stanislavski exercise from Grigorii Dityatkovsky.

**4.6**

# One question behind

GRAMMAR: Assorted interrogative forms
LEVEL: Beginner to intermediate
TIME: 5 – 10 minutes
MATERIALS: One **Question set** for each pair of students

YOU CAN ADAPT THIS BY PREPARING YOUR OWN QUESTION SETS FOR DIFFERENT INTERROGATIVE STRUCTURES

## In class

1 Demonstrate the exercise to your students. Get one of them to ask you the first question of a set. You answer 'Mmmm', with closed lips. The student asks you the second question – you give the answer that would have been right for the first question. The student asks the third question and you reply with the answer to the second question, and so on. The wrong combination of question and answer can be quite funny.
2 Pair the students and give each pair a question set. One student fires the questions and the other gives delayed-by-one replies. The activity is competitive. The first pair to finish a question set is the winner.

---

QUESTION SET A

Where do you sleep? (*the other says nothing*)
Where do you eat? (*the other answers the first question*)
Where do you go swimming?
Where do you wash your clothes?
Where do you read?
Where do you cook?
Where do you listen to music?
Where do you get angry?
Where do you do your shopping?
Where do you sometimes drive to?

© Cambridge University Press 1995

---

LISTENING TO PEOPLE

## QUESTION SET B

What do you eat your soup with? (*the other says nothing*)
What do you cut your meat with? (*the other answers the first question*)
What do you write on?
What do you wipe your mouth with?
What do you blow your nose with?
What do you brush your hair with?
What do you sleep on?
What do you write with?
What do you wear in bed?
What do you wear in church/temple/mosque?

## QUESTION SET C

Can you tell me something you ate last week? (*the other says nothing*)
Tell me something you saw last week? (*the other answers the first question*)
Is there something you have come to appreciate recently?
What about something you really want to do next week?
Where have you spent most of this last week?
Where would you have liked to spend this last week?
Where are you thinking of going on holiday?
Where did you last go on holiday?
Which is the best holiday place you have ever been to?

ONE QUESTION BEHIND

## Variation 1

Have students devise their own sets of questions to then be used as above.

## Variation 2

Group the students in fours: One acts as 'time keeper', one as the 'question master' and person 3 and 4 are the 'players'.

The 'question master' fires five rapid questions at player A which she has to answer *falsely*. The 'time keeper' notes the time the questioning takes. The 'question master' fires five similar questions at B, who answers truthfully. The quickest answerer wins. (The problem lies in choosing the right wrong answer fast enough.)

Possible questions:

How old are you?
Where do you live?
Which colour do you like best?
What time is it?
How did you get here?

What time did you get up today?
What did you have for breakfast?
Where does your best friend live?
What sort of music do you dislike?
How many brothers and sisters do you have?

### RATIONALE

In the main exercise and variation 2 both questioner and answerer have to be doing two things at once. Often this leads to them doing each better. The easy mental gymnastics involved in this exercise make very drill-like work palatable.

### ACKNOWLEDGEMENT

We learnt the activity from a TV show 'Losing a Million'.

## 4.7

# Intensive talk

GRAMMAR: Present tenses and language of description
LEVEL: Post beginner to advanced
TIME: 40 – 50 minutes
MATERIALS: None

## In class

1 Pair the students and ask A in each pair to prepare to describe a person she knows well to B. She will have exactly two-and-a-half minutes for the description. B's job is to listen intently but not take notes. You time the speech window.

2 When the time is up, B feeds back to A everything she understood about the person described.

3 Repeat steps 1 and 2, but with B describing a person she knows well, with A listening carefully and then feeding back.

4 Put the pairs into fours – students A, B, A1 and B1. A works with A1 and B works with B1. A and B both speak for two-and-a-half minutes about the person they spoke about in steps 1 and 3 respectively. A1 and B1 listen with attention. A and B *do not* repeat any of the information from their first description. It must all be new stuff in this second round. At the end of the two-and-a-half minutes, A1 and B1 feedback what they have just heard.

5 A1 and B1 both speak for two-and-a-half minutes about the person they spoke about in steps 1 and 3 respectively. Again, they must *not* include old information. A and B feedback what they have just heard.

6 A1 and B compare what they have heard about A's person and B1's person. A and B1 compare what they have heard about B's person and A1's person.

By the end of this exercise you have doubled the number of people around in the room, or rather, each four has become aware of four more people.

INTENSIVE TALK

# 4.8 Two against the group

| | |
|---|---|
| GRAMMAR: | Past interrogatives (at high speed) |
| LEVEL: | Lower intermediate to advanced |
| TIME: | 3 minutes in first class |
| | 15 – 30 minutes in second class |
| MATERIALS: | None |

## In first class

For homework ask one student to tell another student of their choice a personal story. It needs to be a light-hearted one. The second student should be able to tell it fluently to the group. Maybe they need to hear it twice. (This homework is just for these two members of the class.)

## In second class

1 Ask the two 'story' students to come and sit facing the group.
2 The second student, the one who has heard the story from her partner, will tell the story to the group. The group's job is to stop the telling by asking the first student, whose story it is, as many detailed questions as possible. The questions can be sensible or otherwise, but they must be on the text. The first student must answer all the questions asked.
 The group's aim is to hold up the telling as long as possible while the pair's aim is to disarm the group and get a hearing.
3 During the telling–questioning phase, note down all the faulty questions asked on a transparency. Do *not* correct during the question – answer – telling flow.
4 Put the questions that need grammar attention up on the board and have the learners correct them.

### RATIONALE

The two students at the front in this activity support each other and the interplay between them can be riveting to watch and listen to. The fact that there is so much going on psychologically makes this an excellent grammar exercise. The excitement of the game turns down the linguistic monitor and reveals the mistakes that people come out with naturally when they visit an English-speaking country. During the game the learners are no longer on their best behaviour, linguistically. This gives you the chance to do useful remedial work. Especially useful at higher levels.

LISTENING TO PEOPLE

ACKNOWLEDGEMENT

We learnt the idea of *one* student telling a story against a question-firing group, from André Fonck in Belgium. We published this idea in *The Confidence Book*. People in an adult education teacher group in Lewes did the exercise in the Fonck form and then proposed the duet idea, which is that bit better group-dynamically.

## 5.1

# Real time

| | |
|---|---|
| GRAMMAR: | Language for telling the time |
| LEVEL: | Beginner to post beginner |
| TIME: | 20 – 40 minutes |
| MATERIALS: | Twelve chairs |

## In class

1 Arrange a circle of twelve chairs, with gaps between the chairs. Put a coat over the back of one of them to indicate twelve o'clock.
2 Have the students standing around outside the circle; ask for two volunteers to go into the circle of chairs.
3 Compare the heights of the two students; the taller one becomes the 'big hand' and the shorter the 'little hand'.
4 The volunteers then sit down on two separate chairs. They (or you) ask 'What's the time?' Students outside the circle shout out the answer. Continue, occasionally changing the students in the centre, until you are happy with the students' time telling and pronunciation.
5 Select a student who is shorter than you and go into the centre with them. Ask the student to sit on a chair and sit down yourself, say, on the edge of the 'one o'clock chair', on the edge nearest the 'two o'clock chair'. If the students say seven or eight minutes past, accept it but indicate that it's not what you really want. Assuming no-one comes up with a suggestion, feed in 'just gone' ('after' etc. is fine too).

6 Practise this until the students have got the idea.

7 By sitting on the other edge of the chair introduce and practise 'almost' (or 'coming up to', 'nearly').

## Follow up

Write on the board: '... time.' Sit on, say, the 'twelve o'clock chair' and say: 'My bedtime'. Have students sit on the other chairs and say what they are for them:

    tea time    dinner time    lunch time    break time    breakfast time
    coffee time    free time    closing time    opening time    play time.

You may like to accept structures which aren't normal collocations: newspaper time, video time etc. If so, write them all on the board and do a classification exercise separating out normal collocations and checking meaning. If you're working in an English-speaking country, a comparison with home-time routines is appropriate here.

### RATIONALE

This exercise offers a combination of 'real language' and movement to stimulate the students' learning of what they might easily see as a boring or childish bit of language. When we've done this exercise with students, they've often been appreciative of the chance to stretch their legs and have commented positively about the utility and authentic feel of phrases like 'half three' 'just gone' 'almost' and 'about'.

### NOTE 1

The language above is British English. American English has its own rich set of time-telling phrases, e.g. 'twenty after', 'a quarter of'.

### NOTE 2

In this exercise, if you want less movement or have a small group, you can use cuisinaire rods instead of chairs.

REAL TIME

## 5.2 Sit down then

GRAMMAR: *Who* + simple past interrogative / Telling the time
LEVEL: Beginner to elementary
TIME: 10 – 20 minutes
MATERIALS: None

## In class

1 Ask everybody to stand up. Tell them you are going to shout out bedtimes. When they hear the time *they* went to bed yesterday, they shout 'I did' and sit down. You start like this:

Who went to bed at two a.m.?       Who went to bed at quarter to two?
Who went to bed at ten to two?      Who went to bed at half past one?

Continue until all the students have sat down. (You may want to introduce your students to the different ways the time is told on either side of the Atlantic.)

2 Get people back on their feet. Ask one of the better students to come out and run the same exercise but this time about when people got up, e.g.:

Who woke up at four thirty this morning?
Who woke up at twenty to five?

3 Repeat with a new question master but asking about shopping, e.g.:

Who went shopping yesterday?
Who went shopping on ... (*day of the week*)

### Variation

For a fuller version of this exercise see *The Confidence Book* (p. 63), by Paul Davis and Mario Rinvolucri.

ACKNOWLEDGEMENT
We learnt this technique in a psychodrama session. Barbara Tregear asked us to sit down when she had hit on our feeling of the moment:
'You're feeling apprehensive, you're feeling sleepy, you're feeling cross.'
We used the exercise in this form during a workshop in Cairo – the following day an inspector told us he had tried it out for teaching the time to twelve-year-olds. Thank you, Barbara and Mohammed.

MOVEMENT AND GRAMMAR

## 5.3

# Do you like your neighbours' words?

GRAMMAR: Present simple questions + short answers
*Ones* (substitute word)
Possessive pronouns

LEVEL: Post beginner

TIME: 45 minutes

MATERIALS: None

## In class

### Stage 1  Memory circle

1 Get the students sitting in circles of about twelve. Ask them to stand up and each think of a new or recently learnt English word. They are to sit down when they've got one; give them a minute or two after which everyone should be sitting. (If you want to revise your coursebook then the students can skim the last couple of units or their notes for a word – not dictionaries, though, because then the vocabulary becomes too difficult.)

2 In each circle one student should say their word and explain what it means, if necessary. You can hover to check pronunciation.

3 The student next to the one who started should say and explain their word and then repeat the first student's word.

4 Continue in order round the circle with each student adding and explaining their word and saying the previous words. The student on the end has a lot to remember but plenty of repetition to help them get it.

### Stage 2  Chair game

1 As the first group finishes, stand in the middle of their circle of chairs.

2 Ask a student 'Do you like your neighbour's word?' If the student answers 'yes' have everyone move one seat to the right. If they answer 'no' ask the supplementary question 'Choose two new ones'. The student should then choose two new ones from the memory circle (words, not names of students). The two students to whom the chosen words belong should then stand up and change seats with the two neighbours. As they are changing you sneak into one of the vacated seats leaving one student stranded in the middle.

3 The student in the middle continues by asking another student if they like their neighbour's word and trying to sneak in as they change seats.

4 Once the game structure is established take your seat out and set up another group. (Although the structure of this game is quite simple it's a good example of a game which is difficult to explain to students but easy to demonstrate.)

5 Finally hover and check they're saying the sentences correctly. Continue until just before the students lose the energy to continue with this 'drill'.

## NOTE

We've found that students usually like to write after this exercise. Offer them the option of making a wordlist or writing the two sentences. If each student in the group takes responsibility for the spelling of their words you don't need to intervene too much.

The memory circle bit of this exercise is good for reinforcing the learning of names near the beginning of a course. Get the students to say, e.g. 'He's Amal and his word's …, you're Odette, your word's …' etc.

## ACKNOWLEDGEMENT

We learnt this exercise from Lonny Gold.

# 5.4

# Turn round quick

GRAMMAR: Irregular verbs
LEVEL: Elementary
TIME: 20 – 30 minutes when you first do the exercise
5 – 10 minutes each subsequent time
MATERIALS: None

## In class

1 Face the students and ask them to stand up. Tell them to mirror what you do with body and voice:
   – you now roar like a lion, clawing the air
   – you blow a kiss with a gracious hand movement
   – you wave goodbye.
2 Ask them to pair off and stand back to back. Tell them you will count to three and on *three* they are to spin round and do one of the three gestures. They must *not* agree beforehand on which one. Their aim is to spontaneously choose the same one as their partner does.
3 Count to three – they spin round. Do this three or four times.
4 Ask the students to change partners. Write on the board:

go      infinitive
went    past
gone    past participle

Wipe the first column from the board and ask them to agree with their partners on a mime to capture the idea of the *infinitive*, a mime to represent the *past* and one they like for the *past participle*.
Make clear that the mimes are to represent the *grammar ideas*, not the meaning of this particular verb. You may have to use mother tongue with elementary students to get the idea across clearly. Give the class enough time to create good mimes.
5 Tell them they are going to play the spinning round game again but this time to practise the parts of some irregular verbs.
You write up another verb on the board and explain the meaning, or give the translation if necessary. They get into the back-to-back position and you give them 'one, two, *three*!' They spin round and do the mime as well as say the correct part of the verb, hoping to have chosen the same word and mime as their partner.
6 Run through a dozen hard irregular verbs this way.

## NOTE

In a way, the most interesting part of this exercise is the way students decide how to choreograph grammar concepts like *infinitive*. In observing their process you may find out interesting things about their inner representations of grammar ideas.

## ACKNOWLEDGEMENT

This is an adaptation to grammar work of a Neuro-Linguistic Programming (NLP) exercise we learnt at the 1993 Society for Effective and Affective Learning (SEAL) Conference.

MOVEMENT AND GRAMMAR

## 5.5

# Only if …

GRAMMAR: Polite requests, *-ing* participle
*Only if* + target verb structure of your choice
LEVEL: Elementary +
TIME: 15 – 20 minutes
MATERIALS: None

THIS ACTIVITY IS PARTICULARLY
SUITABLE FOR YOUNG LEARNERS

## In class

1 Make or find as much space in you room as possible and ask the class to stand at one end of it.
2 Explain that their end is one river bank and the opposite end of the room is the other bank. Between is the 'golden river' and you are the 'keeper' of the golden river. Before crossing the river the students have to say the following sentence:

Can we cross your golden river, sitting in your golden boat?

They need to be able to say this sentence reasonably fluently.
3 Get the students to say the sentence. You answer:

Only if you're wearing …
Only if you've got …
Only if you've got … on you.

Supposing you say 'Only if you've got your keys on you'. All the students who have their keys can 'boat' across the 'river' without hindrance. The others have to try to sneak across without being tagged by you. The first person who is tagged, changes places with you and becomes 'it' (the keeper who tags the others in the next round).
4 Continue with students saying 'Can we cross your golden river, sitting in your golden boat?' 'It' might say, 'Only if you're not wearing earrings.' etc.

## Variation 1

To make this game more lively, instead of having just one 'it', everyone who is tagged becomes 'it'. Repeat until everyone has been tagged. Elect another keeper and repeat.

This exercise can be used with various other structures:

    Only if you've been …

    Only if you've been / you went …

    Providing you're going to …

    Providing you were -ing at about six last night / between six and eight last night etc.

## Variation 2

It can also be used to introduce or practise specific structures in a
controlled way by giving the keeper prepared cards, e.g. for the passive use
of *had*:
... your hair cut in the last week.
... your shoes mended recently.
... your bike repaired this month.
... a part of your body pierced.
etc.

### NOTE

This game is one of a few in this book which can be a bit rough. With a
mature class we ask the students at the beginning to 'take responsibility for
their own personal safety' which means we don't have to and (so far, touch
wood) has prevented anything worse than a small bruise. With children,
restricted space or large classes (and also very small classes) having one
continually changing keeper, as in the first version, gives a clearer and
gentler structure to the game.

### ACKNOWLEDGEMENT

A version of this and similar games that can be adapted for language work
are in *Games, Games, Games*, a Woodcraft Folk handbook which is sold in
Oxfam shops in the UK. The Woodcraft Folk are a co-operative, co-
educational UK youth organisation; various games from youth clubs are
suitable for language work.

## 5.6

# Future chairs

GRAMMAR: **Future forms**
LEVEL: **Lower intermediate**
TIME: **30 minutes**
MATERIALS: **None**

THIS ACTIVITY CAN BE ADAPTED
FOR USE WITH OTHER
GRAMMATICAL STRUCTURES

## In class

1 Have three chairs spaced out in front of the class:

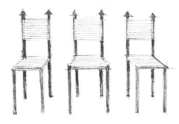

2 Tell the students that the three chairs represent the present continuous,
*going to* and *'ll* ways of expressing the future (see note 1 below). Each
chair represents one of the grammar forms.

3 Give a few real examples from your life sitting in the appropriate chair.
For example, sit on the first chair and say:

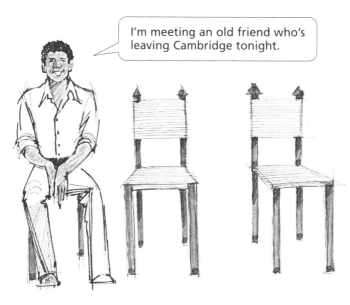

I'm meeting an old friend who's
leaving Cambridge tonight.

MOVEMENT AND GRAMMAR

You then move on to the next chair and say, e.g. 'we're going to go out for a meal,' and on to the third chair and say, e.g. 'then we'll go back for a coffee or go for a drink'.

4 Leave the empty chairs and invite students to come and sit in a chair and say a sentence when they feel like it. Supposing a student says 'I'm doing my homework tonight', fire a couple of concept questions ('you've fixed an exact time? you won't change your mind?' etc.) to check they're in the right chair. If their answers show they're not sitting in the right place, move them and get them to come up with the right sentence for what they're thinking, e.g. 'I'll probably do some homework tonight'. (If you find students are sticking to one structure, it's worth introducing the rule that no chair can be used more than twice consecutively.)

### NOTE 1

Most textbooks and exams treat the three futures used in the exercise above, so it's worth doing exercises like this although there are many grey areas. When we've asked native speakers what they're doing tonight, they've most often answered in one of four ways:

a) Future continuous, e.g. 'I'll be going down the pub'.

b) An *-ing* form with elipsis, e.g. 'Going out' which does not distinguish between the present continuous and the future continuous.

c) A noun or noun phrases, e.g. 'The pub'.

d) A modal, e.g. 'I might go down the pub'.

It's worth doing this exercise again with more than three chairs.

### NOTE 2

This exercise can be adapted easily to other structures, e.g. present continuous for 'around now' versus present tense, various types of conditionals, modals etc.

Both students and the teacher are given a clear insight into how far the structures have been absorbed by doing this exercise.

The 'Body tense map' (2.7) can also usefully be done with chairs.

### ACKNOWLEDGEMENT

See John Morgan's empty chair exercise in *The Recipe Book* edited by Seth Lindstromberg. See also *The Confidence Book* (6.1), by Paul Davis and Mario Rinvolucri for more help in dealing with the future.

FUTURE CHAIRS

**5.7**

# If + present perfect

GRAMMAR: *If* + present perfect
*I'd like you to* + infinitive
Past interrogative

LEVEL: Elementary to intermediate

TIME: 15 – 20 minutes

MATERIALS: None

> THIS ACTIVITY CAN BE ADAPTED
> FOR USE WITH A VARIETY OF
> GRAMMATICAL STRUCTURES

## In class

1 Have the group sit in a circle. Have an empty chair next to where you're sitting in the circle.

2 Write on the board:

> If you've been to (*country/town/region*), I'd like you to sit here.

You get the exercise going by sitting next to the empty seat and saying the sentence. Once a person who has been to the place you mentioned is sitting next to you, ask them these two questions:

> When did you visit X?
> Where did you go in X?

3 There will now be an empty chair somewhere else in the circle. Ask one of the two people either side of it to invite someone to sit next to them, by asking the same question you did but changing the place/country. They also ask the two past tense questions. Carry on for fifteen to twenty chair changes.

4 Change the sentence in circulation to:

> If you've eaten …, I'd like you to sit here.

Tell the group to use this sentence the same way as the first one with these two follow-up questions:

> When did you last eat X?
> What was it like?

GRAMMAR NOTE

The pattern drilled above is one of 50 or so conditional structures used in English. It is odd that people go on referring to *three*. How about 'If you didn't eat your pancake, you probably aren't hungry?'

MOVEMENT AND GRAMMAR

## 5.8    If you had the chance

| GRAMMAR: | 'Second' conditional |
|---|---|
| LEVEL: | Intermediate |
| TIME: | 25 minutes |
| MATERIALS: | None |

THIS ACTIVITY CAN BE USED WITH
A VARIETY OF GRAMMATICAL
STRUCTURES AT DIFFERENT LEVELS

## In class

1  Get all the class sitting on chairs in a big circle, you sitting with them.
2  Select a structure to practise or introduce; we've chosen 'Would you … if you had the chance?' for an intermediate class, but many other structures are suitable.

> Anyone who'd go bungee-jumping if they had the chance, move two to the right.

3  Give students the model, e.g.:

Anyone who'd go bungee-jumping if they had the chance, move two to the right.

All those who would, get up and move to the right and sit down on a seat or someone's lap, if the seat is occupied. (As the game proceeds, several people may end up sitting stacked up on top of each other.)

4 Give another four or five sentences:

Anyone who'd fill their house with pets if they had the chance move four to the left.

Anyone who'd go to live on a small island for a couple of years if they had the chance move three to the right.

Anyone who'd have more than one boy or girlfriend if they had the chance move seven to the right.

Anyone who'd never read another book in their life …

etc.

By now you should have various people sitting in twos or threes or fours on each other's laps and some with chairs to themselves.

5 Hand over the calling-out of the pattern sentences to the students. Any student can chip in a sentence when they feel like it. (You correct when they stray from the structure you've introduced.)

6 When the students have got on top of the structure, slip in fresh but similar structures:

Anyone who'd jump at the chance of …, move …

Anyone who does … if they have the chance, move …

RATIONALE

Perhaps the students for whom this kind of movement exercise is most vital are mid-teenagers. They come to class with bags of physical energy that needs an outlet. This sort of exercise gives it a productive one. We have had problems with teenagers who sometimes find this kind of work childish. The way we've dealt with this successfully is to negotiate or ask permission. We've found that by saying 'do you mind doing something pretty silly?' we've often got a positive response. However, you do have to have an alternative exercise to do if you are refused permission to do the planned activity.

A piece of received wisdom, which we were taught when training to be teachers, was that other cultures and subcultures such as Arabs and business people would not like physical games. Once, when one of us had two head-scarfed, Saudi women in a multilingual, co-educational class we broke a self-imposed taboo and checked with them – these two gave permission and joined in the movement game above with gusto. Business people always seem to enjoy games, so we've stopped even asking. They certainly appreciate the validity of an appropriate game presented in a proper frame and for a clear language-learning and mood-modifying aim.

MOVEMENT AND GRAMMAR

# 5.9 Moving Ludo (Pachisi)

| | |
|---|---|
| GRAMMAR: | Varied |
| LEVEL: | Intermediate |
| TIME: | 60 minutes |
| MATERIALS: | Twenty pieces of paper per group of six students |
| | Photocopies of **Sentence sheets**, one per three students |

## Preparation

Prepare sheets of sentences, some correct and some wrong (see examples below). Photocopy one per three students. Number blank sheets of A4 paper 1–10, a set for each three students and a sheet labelled 'home' per six students.

## In class

1 The class should be divided into groups of six. Each group lays out a simplified ludo board as below on the floor:

2 Divide students on each board into two groups of three. Give out copies of the **Sentence sheets**. One group of three gets **Sentence sheet 1**, the other gets **Sentence sheet 2**. Students stand on 'home'.

3 One of the students from the first team is given a sentence by the other team. The student has to say if the sentence is *right* or *wrong*, and if it's wrong, correct it.

A *right* answer is *forward two steps* round the board.

A *wrong* answer is *back two*. *A correction* of a sentence is a *bonus* of *two*. If the student needs to *consult* the other members of the team, a *right* answer is *forward one*.

Once the student has given an answer, the six students negotiate whether it's right or wrong consulting you as a referee if disputes occur.

4 The other two members of the first team are given sentences.

5 When all three members of the first team have been given a sentence then each member of the other team is asked in turn.

6 The teams take turns for each person to answer a question. The first team with all three members back 'home' after a circuit is the winner.

---

SENTENCE SHEET 1

1  He had had whisky before.
2  Seen any good films lately?
3  I do like English, don't you?
4  Have you got used to speaking English yet?
5  I do make some mistakes.
6  She's gone to the cinema yesterday.
7  I'm going, are you?
8  If you were him you'd do it.
9  I am used to go to school by bus when I was a child.
10  I'm having a bath every day.
11  I love to hate it.
12  Please forgive me for being so rude last time we have met.
13  Do you go to the cinema tomorrow?
14  I'm going home early.

© Cambridge University Press 1995

---

MOVEMENT AND GRAMMAR

## SENTENCE SHEET 2

1  Doesn't know what she's talking about.
2  I'd like visiting you home very much.
3  If I were you I wouldn't eat that.
4  Can you tell me what means this word?
5  I did do it.
6  I like any pop music.
7  Nice to see you both – did you meet each other in town?
8  Excuse me, is there a possibility to have a meal?
9  He told that it was impossible.
10  She's a very interested person.
11  Last time we have met we had a good time.
12  He'd done it before.
13  I'd like some more.
14  If you see her say hello, will you?

© Cambridge University Press 1995

RATIONALE

The format of this game means that, if an individual can't get an answer, it reverts to the whole team to pick up points. All members of a team must finish. Cooperation within the team is necessary and so makes this an ideal activity with multi-level classes. It's worth thinking of making up teams of a weak student, an average student and a strong student.

# 6.1

# Iffy sentences

| | |
|---|---|
| GRAMMAR: | Varied |
| LEVEL: | Upper intermediate to advanced |
| TIME: | 30 – 40 minutes |
| MATERIALS: | One batch of **Iffy sentences** (for dictation) per lesson (there are enough **Iffy sentences** supplied for four lessons) |

## In class

1 Ask the students to turn their pages longways and to rule three columns with these headings:

Meaningful     Iffy     Meaningless

Explain that you are going to dictate around a dozen sentences. Their task is to decide whether the sentences are fully meaningful, completely without meaning or in an in-between category (doubtful or iffy). Tell them to write the sentence down in the column that corresponds to their decision.

2 As a trial run give them this sentence:

If it's eleven then it's ten.

Ask different students which column they would put the sentence in. Students who contextualise it as referring to time zones will probably find it meaningful.

3 Now dictate the sentences in **Iffy sentences** Batch 1. Read each sentence, pause and read it again so the students have time to make their semantic, contextualising decisions.

4 Group the students in threes to explain to each other why they placed each sentence the way they did.

5 Get the whole class together and ask them to share their semantic judgements of three or four sentences.

### IFFY SENTENCES BATCH 1

1 I'm sorry I'm not here.
2 Ring Mary, her husband used to be Syrian.
3 She made me a father.
4 Shut up so I can hear you!
5 All my friends are priests but I don't have any friends.
6 He made me a father.

7  She's got twin sisters who are a year older than she is.
8  Too much is not quite enough.
9  Could I have a little less water in my coffee please?
10  He didn't want to have his bath again.
11  The woman who has two studies always does her best work in the other one.
12  I am angry with him for having what I gave him.
13  Oh God, may I be alive when I die!

---

## COMMENTARY ON **IFFY SENTENCES** BATCH 1.

*This is a commentary, not a key. You and your students may have quite different feelings about the sentences and be just as 'right' as us.*

1  An apology for being mentally absent or an ansaphone message.
2  Either Mary used to have a husband or he used to be Syrian before changing his nationality.
3  Either the speaker is male and they had a child together or the speaker was the adopted child of two lesbians, one of whom acted in a fatherly way.
4  Logically meaningless but exactly what a teacher may say to a rowdy class.
5  We feel this one is meaningless. Can you find a context where it makes sense? Could the speaker be violently anti-clerical?
6  He acted towards me as a father.
7  The speaker is not herself a triplet.
8  Logically meaningless and yet it could describe some work ethics, maybe.
9  Is this a polite way of complaining, a rather clever reframing?
10  Iffy: is having your bath again and having a second bath the same thing?
11  So she never does her best work!
12  The sentence makes sense in so far as there are people who make gifts and then regret doing it.
13  The speaker could be thinking about not wanting to be a vegetable on his deathbed or could be thinking about the afterlife.

## IFFY SENTENCES BATCH 2

1 Well, the man's broken all his legs.
2 My toothbrush is pregnant again.
3 When we want your opinion, we'll give it to you.
4 I went out robbing to buy friends.
5 The EC has forced Spain to voluntarily reduce its dairy consumption.
6 The answer will have black hair.
7 I was happily glossed over.
8 My sister is in Paris for three weeks; she's going back to Canterbury tomorrow.
9 These ideas have been asleep for several years now.
10 I forbid you to go out again if you don't come back.
11 It's going to be tomorrow soon.

## IFFY SENTENCES BATCH 3

1 Somebody dropped out next Tuesday so we stepped in.
2 Scientists believe the UK is about to take the lead in averting computer-aided disasters.
3 I did this course fourteen evenings a week.
4 A judge has sentenced James Thompson to be executed twice and fined $200,000 for killing some of his in-laws.
5 I'm never going to amount to much.
6 Finding the money for some people is far from easy.
7 Shall we invite husbands or boyfriends?
8 Britain's roads are becoming less dangerous but more deadly.
9 You'll fail, providing you prepare inadequately.
10 Experts expect no more than a decline in the acceleration of house prices in London.
11 Sterility may be inherited.

## IFFY SENTENCES BATCH 4

1 Shoes are required to eat in the restaurant.
2 She made me a mother.
3 I don't want him to get into the water until he has learnt to swim.
4 Try not to be more nasty than you can avoid.
5 If my grandmother were alive now she'd turn in her grave.
6 I think she must have enjoyed it horribly.
7 Write down three things you don't know about the other person.
8 Katie has developed an innate sense of justice.
9 I've lost my umbrella here and it isn't even mine.
10 He knows everything and he's not interested in anything else.

MEANING AND TRANSLATION

## RATIONALE

This is one of the most powerful intensive reading exercises that we know of (at sentence level). In some of the sentences, grammar and syntax play a major part in the interpretation. In making sense of 'Ring Mary, her husband used to be Syrian' students have to understand the weight of *used to* as habitual past that no longer describes the situation. They also have to figure out whether *used to* refers to nationality or marital status. (Most of the sentences we offer for this exercise are taken from real speech or real writing.) It is odd that there are so many exercises in EFL that ask students to make judgements about areas like phonology and grammar, but very few that ask them to make judgements about meaning. Most people have strong opinions about meaning, especially their own mapping of it.

## FURTHER MATERIAL

You will find more **Iffy sentences** in *Dictation* (5.2), by Paul Davis and Mario Rinvolucri.

## 6.2 Two-faced sentences

GRAMMAR: Varied – special emphasis on syntax
LEVEL: Upper intermediate to very advanced
TIME: 30 – 45 minutes
MATERIALS: One batch of **Two-facers** (for dictation) per lesson (there are enough **Two-facers** supplied for six lessons)

## In class

1 Tell the students you are going to dictate ten short sentences to them in English. They are to take them down in their mother tongue. Dictate the sentences twice each. Pause briefly between each reading to give them translation time, but don't let the rhythm get saggy. Do not dictate the notes you will find in brackets – these are for you, the teacher.

2 Put the students in groups of four to compare their translations. (If you teach people with various mother tongues, ask the people with 'lone languages' to form a syndicate working together – they will be comparing their readings of the English.) It may be worth pointing out that some of the sentences are several-faced, not just two-faced.

3 Go through the more complex of the sentences with the whole group. It is only very advanced learners who will get all three meanings of, e.g. 'It was sighted/cited/sited in Hannover.'

### TWO-FACERS BATCH 1

1 The teacher told the student she had failed. *(Who does 'she' refer to?)*
2 She missed him. *(at the meeting place, because of absence, because she was a bad shot)*
3 It was sighted/cited/sited in Hannover. *(a bird, a text or a building)*
4 It is a myth that one needs to develop. *(Is the need for further development a myth or should this myth be developed further?)*
5 I don't interview particularly well. *(passive or active?)*
6 He is the second senior politician to be killed in Northern Ireland. *(Does 'second' qualify 'senior' or 'senior politician'?)*
7 No five fingers are really alike. *(Is the comparison within a set of five or between sets of five?)*
8 Mary thinks of John with nothing on. *(Who is naked?)*

MEANING AND TRANSLATION

9   To be fair, Tom divided the sweets equally. *(Does the adverbial phrase refer to the division of the sweets or to the speaker's attitude to Tom?)*

10  I'm going to have these blown up. *(a military commander speaking of homes in a territory he is occupying, or a photographer?)*

## TWO-FACERS BATCH 2

1   I've read a lot recently on trains. *(Does 'on' indicate place or mean 'about'?)*

2   The singer was upset when she booked him. *(Who does 'she' refer to? Agents book singers and, in British English, so do traffic wardens and police women.)*

3   Everybody likes his mother. *(whose?)*

4   Do men sell better than women in Japan? *(Is 'sell' active or passive?)*

5   Shall I hold him for you? *(in the flesh or on the phone?)*

6   What an idiot I am to teach! *(Am I a poor learner or was I a fool to take up teaching or am I thinking about the future?)*

7   No one thought more of the Italians than the French. *(Are the French the subject of the sentence or the object of the comparison?)*

8   There is nothing I like more than beating foreigners. *(skinhead or sportsman?)*

9   WOMEN OFFER TO TAKE ATTACKER OUT [headline] *(to date with them or to kill them?)*

10  She's got to like him. *(semi-modal or present perfect?)*

## TWO-FACERS BATCH 3

1   She taught her daughter everything she knew. *(everything who knew?)*

2   I was over working in Germany. [Don't dictate this one, write it up.] *(working in Germany for a time or working too hard?)*

3   What she has just told you is practically true. *(Does 'practically' mean 'virtually' or 'for practical purposes'?)*

4   EGYPTIAN POLICE RING UNIVERSITY [headline] *('telephone' or 'surround'?)*

5   If the baby won't drink the milk, boil it. *(What does 'it' refer to?)*

6   We've never had this sort of post before. *(Does 'post' mean 'mail' or 'job position' or 'post in a fence'?)*

7   Why not tell your friend's/friends' story? *(one friend or more?)*

8   Can I have a taxi for five, please? *(number of people or time?)*

9   Our sales consultant is all over the place. *(travels a great deal or is in chaos?)*

10  If you decide to pass him, you may regret it. *(Are you an examiner or a driver?)*

## TWO-FACERS BATCH 4

1 The lawyer had totally mismanaged his affairs. *(business or love?)*
2 Both my kids wear braces. *(for their teeth or to hold their trousers up?)*
3 Accounting for growth is not always easy. *(Does 'accounting' mean 'to do accountancy work' or 'to explain'?)*
4 He's got the Tories to attack. *(Is 'he's got' present tense or present perfect?)*
5 The Association has a million odd members. [Write this one, don't dictate it.] *(approximately a million or a million strange members?)*
6 She left instructions for me to follow. *(Was I to follow her or the instructions?)*
7 SACKED TEACHER WINS HEARING [headline] *(Did she manage to get her case to court or did she win the case?)*
8 They saw the drunk down the passageway. *(Did they accompany him or did they see him in the distance?)*
9 Is he on the phone? *(Does he have a phone or is he using it now?)*
10 Please stagger coming into lunch. *(Does 'stagger' mean 'come at different times' or 'walk unsteadily'?)*

## TWO-FACERS BATCH 5

1 I always thought I would have four children from a very early age. *(What does 'from a very early age' refer to?)*
2 John passed the hammer and saw through the window. *(Is 'saw' a noun or a verb?)*
3 It's too easy to forget it. *(Does 'too easy' refer to 'it' or to forgetting?)*
4 Too much change can weigh you down. *(coins or alterations?)*
5 Starving people can sometimes be wrong. *(Is 'starving' a noun or an adjective?)*
6 Do you know what they have to spend a month? $5,000. *(Does 'have to' imply availability or obligation?)*
7 Could you use an action plan? *(Would you know how to, or would one be useful?)*
8 We met them leaving the room. *(Who was leaving?)*
9 I've got six exams in eight days. *(within this period or in eight days' time?)*
10 It could be yours. *(Is this an invitation or a statement of doubt?)*

MEANING AND TRANSLATION

## TWO-FACERS BATCH 6

1  I'm sorry to bother you two/too. *('both' or 'as well')*
2  The word ewe/you/yew can have more than one meaning.
3  I used to have forgotten things. [Don't dictate this one, write it.] *(Is 'forgotten' part of the verb phrase or is it an adjective qualifying 'things'?)*
4  Poor people like us. *(What part of speech is 'like'?)*
5  Nobody looked harder than Mrs Thatcher. *(Is 'harder' an adjective or an adverb?)*
6  Funding chaos can be productive. *(Is 'funding' a noun or an adjective?)*
7  I've had my bike stolen. *(Was it by chance or did you organise it?)*
8  The suspicions of politicians run deep. *(Who is suspicious of who?)*
9  I'll tell you if you're good. *(Is being good a condition for being told or is it what you are told about?)*
10  I simply can't do your things as well as mine. *(Does 'as well as' mean 'too' or does it mean 'in as satisfactory a way as'?)*

## Variation

Instead of asking students to listen to ambiguous sentences and translate them, ask them to envision them and then write very brief notes about what they saw or felt. This quite different exercise is even more deliciously multi-meaningful than the translation exercise.

### RATIONALE

We feel that awareness of ambiguity is a useful state of mind both in mother and target tongues. It is also a mind-opening way of helping advanced students to focus on grammar, semantics and contextualisation (pragmatics, if you like technical terms).

### NOTE

Collecting ambiguous sentences is fun in any language – do any such sentences come to mind in languages that you know other than English? Why not organise a school competition in mother tongue and in English?

### ACKNOWLEDGEMENT

The variation above is Peta Gray's. She co-wrote *Letters*, by Nicky Burbidge et al. You will find more batches of such sentences in *Dictation*, by Paul Davis and Mario Rinvolucri.

## 6.3    Grammar homophones

| | |
|---|---|
| GRAMMAR: | Revision of irregular verbs |
| LEVEL: | Intermediate to advanced |
| TIME: | 20 minutes homework and 20 – 30 minutes in class |
| MATERIALS: | Table of irregular verbs per student |
| | One copy per student of **One child's World War II** text |

## In first class

Ask the students to read **One child's World War II** for homework and to correct all the wrong spellings.

---

### ONE CHILD'S WORLD WAR II

I was born and bread in North Wales. When Italy declared wore on Britain, my father, who was Italian, was scent to a British concentration camp on the Isle of Man where he spent from 1940 to 1943. My mother took me to visit him every six months and maybe my first memory was that I through my teddy bear at the British officer who was always present when they met. I no this maid my parents laugh!

I think my father rote to my Mum once a month, but this is hazy.

Like many Second World War children, I was tolled that if I eight carrots I would really be able to sea in the dark. The problem was I couldn't bare the taste of carrots.

In spring 1943 the Italian Government decided to flea Rome. Italy changed sides in the war and my Dad one his freedom. By then I had groan into a sturdy three-year-old and when I herd from my Mum that he was coming back I was gob-smacked. We had a honeymoon period, him and me.

When I was four I court whooping cough and very nearly dyed of it. I remember the way the cough would sheik my whole body. I remember how I would moan and groan at night. Somehow I new inside that I was very ill. The cough had warn me out.

Anyway I did recover and am here today to tell you the tail!

© Cambridge University Press 1995

---

MEANING AND TRANSLATION

# In second class

1 Put the students in threes to compare their corrections and to pool the meanings of the words used in place of the irregular verbs.
2 Draw the class together to check that they have discovered the meanings of words like 'flea', 'to dye' and 'to toll'.
3 Give them an irregular verb table (or ask them to refer to the one in their textbook) and ask if they can see/hear any more homophones, e.g. blew/blue, read/red, sought/sort, sewn/sown.

ACKNOWLEDGEMENT
We learnt the application of homophone thinking to irregular verbs in R. Jordan's 'Short Storey' that appeared in the January 1993 issue of *Modern English Teaching*.
This exercise and the one on homophones and associations in *Dictation* by Paul Davis and Mario Rinvolucri, strongly affect people who live a lot in the world of vision.

## 6.4 Written conversations

| | |
|---|---|
| GRAMMAR: | Varied |
| LEVEL: | Elementary to advanced |
| TIME: | 30 – 40 minutes |
| MATERIALS: | None |

THE EXERCISE IS DESIGNED FOR A CLASS THAT SHARES THE SAME MOTHER TONGUE; SEE THE VARIATION FOR MULTILINGUAL CLASSES

## In class

1 Get the students up and milling around and then ask them to choose someone they feel like working with.
2 Tell them they are going to have two parallel written conversations with their partner which will go this way:
  – Both students write the first line of the conversation they are initiating. They write in English. They do this silently.
  – They swap papers and translate what the other person has written into mother tongue. They then write their answer in mother tongue.
  – They swap papers again – each translates what the other has written into English and then replies in English.
  If the students' mother tongue is French the beginning of one side of one of the two written conversations could look like this:
  (in student A's writing)                     'What are we supposed to do?'
  (in student B's writing – translation)   'Qu'est-ce-qu'on doit faire?'
  (in student B's writing – reply)           'On s'écrit.'
  (in student A's writing – translation)   'We write to each other.'
  (in student A's writing – reply)           'What are you doing this evening?'
  etc.
  You need to be everywhere giving translation help and help with direct writing in English.
3 Tell the students to come together in sixes and read each others' dialogues.

## Variation

Do the exercise as set out above but intralingually. Instead of translating, the students paraphrase in English. This is an excellent way of inviting intermediate students to enrich their expression.

MEANING AND TRANSLATION

## RATIONALE

In doing this exercise, students come to see how similar and how different the grammars of their mother tongue and English actually are.

This is a counselling, 'good listening/reading' exercise since you are not allowed to give your reply until you have paraphrased what the other person has written. It's excellent for groups where people don't pay too much attention to one another.

It is a gem of a translation exercise, as you have the author of what you are translating there at your elbow. You are translating within a living relationship and you are a protagonist rather than a third party, as is the case in an interpreting situation.

## NOTE

This exercise only works well if each pair of students is engaged in two parallel dialogues. If they only write one, there is a lot of time spent doing nothing.

## ACKNOWLEDGEMENT

The exercises above derive from Dierk Andresen's beautifully simple, written dialogue exercise. He pairs the students and asks both partners to write this sentence: 'some people like the colour blue'. They swap papers and write their separate, individual responses to this statement. They swap papers again and react to each other's reactions and so on. Thank you Dierk!

## NOTE ON ORAL TRADITION

EFL methodology is a mixture of written transfer of ideas and of oral transmission. We learnt the Andresen technique in a workshop where he demonstrated it. He may have thought it up himself or learnt it from somewhere else. As is normal in the oral tradition, we do not remember back beyond the person who taught us. Teachers who read this page may try out the ideas and find they work. The ideas, probably enriched and transformed, then become part of their bag of tricks. They may well pass them on to other colleagues, one of whom then writes a book in which another transformation of the ideas resurfaces. And so on.

# 6.5 The world of take

GRAMMAR: Some basic meanings of the verb *take*, in particle verbs
LEVEL: Intermediate to advanced
TIME: 40 – 50 minutes
MATERIALS: Set of sentences below (for dictation)

## In class

1 Put the students in small groups to brainstorm all the uses of the verb *take* they can think of.
2 Ask each group to send a messenger to the next group to pass on their ideas.
3 Dictate the sentences below which they are to write down in their mother tongue. Tell them only to write in mother tongue, not English. Be ready to help explain any sentences that students do not understand.

1 The new president took over in January.
2 The man took the woman's anger seriously.
3 'You haven't done the washing up, I take it,' his wife said to him.
4 The little boy took the old watch apart to see how it worked.
5 'I think we ought to take the car,' he said to her.
6 This bloke always takes his problems to his mother.
7 'We took the village without a shot being fired,' she told him.
8 'Take care,' the woman said, as she left home that morning.
9 He took charge of the planning team.
10 The woman asked what size shoes he took.
11 'Yes, I really take your point,' he told her.
12 'If we go to a movie,' she told her boyfriend, 'it'll really take you out of yourself.'
13 The news the boy brought really took the woman aback.
14 The chair asked him to take the minutes of the meeting.
15 'You can take it from me, it's worse than you think.'

4 Ask the students to work in threes and compare their translations. Go round helping and checking. If your students do not share the same mother tongue, group students from the same language or language groups. In this sort of class you will probably have three or four people from unrelated languages working together, as well. They learn a lot about each other's languages from this exercise.

MEANING AND TRANSLATION

5 Check that they are clear about the usual direct translation of *take* into their language. Now ask them to mark all the translations where *take* is not rendered by its direct equivalent. (This stage is especially interesting in an international group when people get to compare the behaviours of different mother tongues.)

THE WORLD OF TAKE

## 6.6 Coherence poems

GRAMMAR: Juxtaposition and coherence as the main syntactic feature
LEVEL: Elementary to advanced
TIME: 30 – 40 minutes
MATERIALS: One **Word jumble sheet** for each student
One **Poem sheet** for each student

## In class

1 Ask the students to sit comfortably and do a short relaxation exercise. They shut their eyes and measure a minute in any way they like. At the end of their individual minute they silently raise their hands and open their eyes. (This is a useful calming down and centring device used by Maria Montessori with three-year-olds.)

2 Ask the students to shut their eyes again. Read them the first poem below, very slowly. It is a special kind of poem called a *haiku*. Read it a second time. They open their eyes and you write the poem on the board. Very gently question them to find out what feelings, sounds, smells and pictures the *haiku* has evoked. There are often marvellous differences as they tell you *their* poems, in the way they have perceived the text you read. Repeat with the other two poems below:

1 The year's rain     a grass roof's first leak
2 Snow melting     beggar town's thin children
3 Today too     life in a little house

3 Give the students the **Word jumble sheet** and ask them to produce a *haiku* from each jumble. They can only use the words given in the jumble. Let them work on their own or in pairs, as they choose.

4 The students compare poems.

5 Give out the **Poem sheet**. They read and compare.

RATIONALE

This exercise has students working on the way word juxtaposition, with minimal grammar features, will usefully build sentences. It practises language coherence rather than cohesion.

The students often produce poems as beautiful as the Issa translations, and to do this in the target language gives some people a confidence boost.

MEANING AND TRANSLATION

## WORD JUMBLE SHEET

1   in
mist   the
farewell
lost   hands
farewell
waving

2   homeless
dawn   love   cat
a   crying
too   for   at

3   dirty   wife
but   has   yes

a    the
cat

4   at   up
the   a
sky
frog
scowling
evening

5   rain
crows
pigeons   spring
mating   mating

6   crapping
prayer
even
nightingale
the
sings
a

7  butterfly
meadow
a
reborn
be
to
bliss

8   in
priest   butterfly
cat    row
sleeping
a  a  a  a

9   butt   the
big   horse
blossoms   rubs
his
cherry

10   snail   feet
you   when
here
at   did   my
get

POEM SHEET

1 Farewell farewell      hands waving lost in the mist
2 At dawn homeless too      a cat crying for love
3 Dirty yes      but the cat has a wife
4 Scowling up at the evening sky      a frog
5 Pigeons mating      crows mating      spring rain
6 Even crapping      the nightingale sings a prayer
7 Bliss to be reborn a meadow butterfly
8 Sleeping in a row      a butterfly      a cat      a priest
9 The big horse rubs his butt      cherry blossoms
10 At my feet      when did you get here      snail

ACKNOWLEDGEMENT

The poems above are taken from *Issa, Cup of Tea Poems, Selected Haiku of Kobayashi Issa*, Asian Humanities Press, 1991.

MEANING AND TRANSLATION

# 6.7

# Two-word verbs

GRAMMAR: Compound verbs
LEVEL: Upper intermediate to advanced
TIME: 40 – 50 minutes
MATERIALS: One **Mixed-up verb sheet** per pair of students
The **Jumbled sentences** on an OHP transparency or each sentence written on a large separate piece of card

## In class

1 Pair the students and ask them to match the verbs on the **Mixed-up verb sheet** you give them. Tell them to use dictionaries and to call you over. Be everywhere at once.

2 Ask them to take a clean sheet of paper and a pen or pencil suitable for drawing. Tell them you are going to give them a few phrases to illustrate. They are to draw a situation that brings out the meaning of the phrases. Here are the phrases – do not give them more than 30 seconds per drawing (they will groan):

to toilet-train a child
to soft-soap a superior
to force-feed an anorexic
to court-martial a soldier
to back-comb a person's hair
to cross-examine a witness
to spin-dry your clothes
to cold-shoulder a friend

3 Give them time to compare their drawings. The drawings often make misunderstandings manifest.

4 Split the class into teams of four. Tell them you are going to show them jumbled sentences (see below) and their task will be to shout out the unjumbled sentence. The first team to shout out a correct sentence gets a point.

### NOTE

This exercise is an example of what you can do with the very useful, grammatically classified lists of words to be found in the *Collins COBUILD English Grammar*, edited by John Sinclair. Since the grammar is corpus-based, we can teach students the most usual compound verbs.

**135**

## MIXED-UP VERB SHEET

*Please match words from column 1 with words from column 2 to form correct compound verbs.*

| *Column 1* | *Column 2* |
|---|---|
| back- | dry |
| cross- | soap |
| ghost- | treat |
| soft- | write |
| blow- | reference |
| double- | cross |
| ill- | dry |
| spin- | comb |
| | |
| cold- | manage |
| double- | feed |
| pooh- | read |
| spoon- | pooh |
| court- | glaze |
| dry- | clean |
| proof- | shoulder |
| stage- | martial |
| | |
| frog- | march |
| wrong- | record |
| toilet- | foot |
| tape- | train |
| short- | change |
| rubber- | feed |
| force- | stamp |
| field- | test |
| cross- | question |
| cross- | examine |
| cross- | check |

© Cambridge University Press 1995

MEANING AND TRANSLATION

## JUMBLED SENTENCES

WILL STILL CAN YOU AND IT IT DRY RETAIN ITS SPIN SHAPE
You can spin-dry it and it will still retain its shape.

COLD HIM WE SHOULDERED FIRST AT
At first we cold-shouldered him.

OUR ILL ANCESTORS TREATED THEY
They ill-treated our ancestors.

CLEAN IT DON'T DRY
Don't dry-clean it.

BLACK FROG THEY MARIA TO THE MARCHED HIM
They frog-marched him to the Black Maria.

DOUBLE YOUR WINDOWS GLAZE TO LIKE WE'D
We'd like to double-glaze your windows.

POOH JUST HIS POOHED OFFER THEY
They just pooh-poohed his offer.

DON'T SOAP ME YOU SOFT DARE
Don't you dare soft-soap me!

## ACKNOWLEDGEMENT

The idea in step 4 above is one we learnt from Richard Acklam.

TWO-WORD VERBS

SECTION 7 PROBLEM SOLVING

## 7.1

# The woman on the roof

GRAMMAR: **Present continuous**
LEVEL: **Elementary**
TIME: **30 – 40 minutes**
MATERIALS: **None**

THIS EXERCISE IS SUITABLE
FOR MONOLINGUAL CLASSES –
SEE NOTE BELOW IF YOU
TEACH A MULTILINGUAL CLASS

## In class

1 Tell the students to tear two pages up into twelve slips of paper.
2 Ask them to imagine a woman on a roof. Ask them to shut their eyes and picture her up there on the roof.
3 Now ask them to write up to twelve different reasons why she is on that roof, e.g. 'She's sun-bathing'.
  Each new sentence goes on a different slip of paper. Sentence 1 is in English, sentence 2 is in mother tongue, sentence 3 is in English, sentence 4 is in mother tongue and so on. Make it clear that each sentence is to convey a new meaning. Sentence 2 is *not* a translation of sentence 1. Tell the students to write all the English sentences in the present continuous. The L1 sentences should use the verb-form that expresses the 'here and now' present in that language.

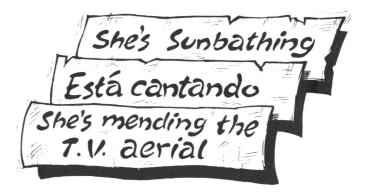

4 As the students write, be everywhere helping and correcting. They will need a great deal of vocabulary. Encourage the use of dictionaries – the right time to learn a word is when the student wants it, not when the teacher wants them to want it.
5 When everybody has got at least eight sentences, have them mill round the room showing their sentences to each other. Their task is to find

PROBLEM SOLVING

either accurate translations of what they have written or semi-translations. Students are amazed to discover that other people have had the same idea but clothed it in the other language. You may or may not want to make it explicit with the students, but they are doing strong contrastive grammar analysis in their search for translations, especially if their mother tongue does not have a form similar to the present continuous.

## NOTE
You can do this exercise successfully in a mixed nationality class. In step 4 above, people from the same language compare sentences. Group any 'lone language' students together. They will have to translate all their mother tongue sentences into English. They may well need your help with this.

# 7.2 Umbrella

| | |
|---|---|
| GRAMMAR: | Modals and present simple |
| LEVEL: | Elementary to intermediate |
| TIME: | 30 – 40 minutes |
| MATERIALS: | One large sheet of paper per student |

## In class

1 Ask a student to draw a picture on the board of a person holding an umbrella. The umbrella looks like this:

Explain to the class that this 'tulip-like' umbrella design is a new, experimental one.

2 Ask the students to work in small groups and brainstorm all the advantages and disadvantages of the design they can see. Ask them to use these sentence stems:

It/You *can/can't* …
It/You + present simple …
It/You *will/won't* …
It/You *may/may not* …

For example: 'It is easy to control in a high wind', 'You can see where you are going with this umbrella'.

3 Give the students large sheets of paper and ask them to list the advantages and disadvantages in two columns.

4 Ask the students to move around the room and read each other's papers. Individually they mark each idea as 'good', 'bad' or 'intriguing'.

5 Ask the students to transfer the sentences marked 'intriguing' to the board. Ask whose sentences these are and what the individuals would like to say about them.

6 Ask each student how many advantages they came up with and how many disadvantages. Ask the students to divide up into three groups according to which statement applies to them:
   - I thought mainly of advantages.
   - I thought of some of both.
   - I thought mainly of disadvantages.

7 Ask the three groups to come up with five to ten adjectives to describe their group state of mind and put these up on the board.

8 Round off the exercise by telling the class that when de Bono asked different groups of people to do this kind of exercise, it turned out that primary school children mostly saw advantages, business people had plenty of both while groups of teachers were the most negative.

## NOTE

Although this exercise may look challenging, the students do come up with the advantages. Here are some of the advantages of the new umbrella that students have come up with:

In a hot country you can collect rain water.

If you go to a political meeting with this umbrella you can see the speaker.

It won't drip round the edges.

You can use it for carrying shopping.

It's not dangerous in a crowd.

It's an optimistic umbrella.

It's easy to hold if two people are walking together.

You may want to use it as a parasol.

It makes you feel tall.

You can use it to protect a plant from the midday sun.

With this umbrella you'll look special.

It'll take less floor space to dry.

You'll get a free supply of ice if it hails.

This umbrella makes people communicate. They can see each other.

You can paint this umbrella to look like a flower.

UMBRELLA

## 7.3

# Eyes

GRAMMAR: 'Second' conditional
LEVEL: Lower to upper intermediate
TIME: 30 – 45 minutes
MATERIALS: None

## In class

1  Ask a student to draw a head in profile on the board. Ask the student to add eyes in the back of this head.
2  Give the students this sentence beginning on the board and ask them to complete it using the grammar suggested:

If people had eyes in the backs of their heads, then they ... *would / 'd / might / could / would have to* ... (+ infinitive).

For example:
'If people had eyes in the backs of their heads they could read two books at once' (so *two* pairs of eyes).

3  Tell the students to write the above sentence stem at the top of their paper and then complete it with fifteen separate ideas. Encourage the use of dictionaries. Help students all you can with vocabulary and go round checking and correcting.
4  Once students have all written a good number of sentences (at least ten) ask them to form teams of four. In the fours they read each other's sentences and pick the four most interesting ones.
5  Each team puts their four best sentences on the board.
6  The students come up to the board and tick the two sentences they find the most interesting. The team that gets the most ticks wins.

NOTE
Students come up with a good range of social, medical and other hypotheses. Here are some examples:
... then they would not need driving mirrors.
... they would make really good traffic wardens.
... then you could kiss someone while looking away!

PROBLEM SOLVING

## 7.4 A dictionary game

| | |
|---|---|
| GRAMMAR: | Comparatives, *it* (referring back) |
| LEVEL: | Elementary (or as a review at higher levels) |
| TIME: | 45 minutes |
| MATERIALS: | One dictionary per two students |

THIS ACTIVITY PROVIDES GOOD SKILLS PRACTICE IN SCAN READING A DICTIONARY

## Preparation

On the board write the following:

a b c d e f g h i j k l m n o p q r s t u v w x y z

It's got more letters than …
It's got fewer letters than …
It's the same length as …
It's earlier in the dictionary than …
It's later in the dictionary than …
It's further on.
Back a bit.
The first letter's right.
The first two/three/four letters are right.

(or you could dictate this to the students if you want a quiet settling-in period at the start of the class)

## In class

1 Explain to the class that you're going out of the room for a short time and they are to select one word for you to guess when you come back. They find the word in their dictionaries.
2 Go back in and have a first wild guess at the class's word. The students should tell you whether their word is longer, shorter or the same length as your guess and whether it's earlier or later in the dictionary. Here is an example (teachers can correct pronunciation as they go along):
TEACHER: Middle.
STUDENTS: It's shorter. And it's later in the dictionary.
TEACHER: Train.

STUDENTS: It's earlier. It's got the same number of letters.
TEACHER: Plane.
STUDENTS: It's later.
TEACHER: Rains.
STUDENTS: It's later. It's got the same number of letters.
TEACHER: Seat.
STUDENTS: It's longer. The first letter is right. It's later in the dictionary.
TEACHER: Stops.
STUDENTS: It's earlier.
TEACHER: Skirt.
STUDENTS: It's later.
TEACHER: Spend.
STUDENTS: The first two letters are right. It's later.
TEACHER: Spine.
STUDENTS: It's later.
TEACHER: Spore.
STUDENTS: The first four letters are right. You're really warm now. It's a bit further on.
TEACHER: Sport.
STUDENTS: Yes.

You can write the words you guess and notes of the students' answers on the board as you go along, to help you to remember where you are. At the beginning, you can prompt the students by asking questions such as 'is it shorter, longer or the same length as my word? is it earlier or later in the dictionary?' etc.

3 When the students have got the idea of the game, reverse the process; you think of a word (one from a recent lesson works well) and students guess. You give them information as to length, place in dictionary and any letters they've guessed right. If, at this stage, you ask the students to have dictionaries handy to scan, this is pretty easy; without a dictionary it's more difficult. Using a recently learnt word and encouraging the students to take notes also makes it easier.

4 Now hand over the exercise to the students. They should scan their notes, textbooks and/or minds (but not dictionaries) and create a short wordlist. Then in pairs or small groups they can repeat the activity.

## RATIONALE

This is a good game for teaching scan reading and alphabetical order when using dictionaries. The revision or introduction of the grammatical structures in a meaningful context is disguised since the students usually see this as a vocabulary game. Because it has a pretty tight structure and build-up, it's a good exercise for establishing the principle of group/pairwork with a class that does not take readily to working in different formats.

PROBLEM SOLVING

This exercise is based on a computer game but it can be done, at least equally well, with people.

**NOTE**

With some classes we have asked the students to analyse their own guessing processes. Some students have written interesting short compositions on the best guessing strategies.

# 7.5 Near future seen from distant future

| | |
|---|---|
| GRAMMAR: | Past perfect and past simple |
| LEVEL: | Intermediate to advanced |
| TIME: | 30 – 40 minutes |
| MATERIALS: | None |

## In class

1 Explain that the year is now 2020. Ask each student to write down their current age (in 2020).
2 Explain that back in the mid-nineties of the last century, scientists invented TV spectacles that allowed you to see things normally and, at the same time, to see a TV picture hanging in space near the edge of your field of vision.
3 Dictate the following sentence stem:

Once they had invented TV specs …

4 Ask the students to complete the sentence between ten and twelve times describing consequences of the invention. Ask them to write each sentence on a separate slip of paper, e.g. 'once they had invented TV specs, security guards could walk round premises while viewing through all the surveillance cameras', 'once they had invented TV specs, drivers viewed TV programmes at the wheel'.
5 Ask the students to get up and mill round the room. Ask them to 'barter' some of their sentences for other sentences they like. They should get at least five new sentences. Make clear they should not give up sentences they like without getting good sentences in return.

NOTE

On 18 September 1993, the *New Scientist* reported the appearance on the market of sports glasses that superimpose T.V. images in a corner of the wearer's normal field of vision. This is quite distinct from virtual reality headsets that take up the whole of the wearer's field of vision.

PROBLEM SOLVING

## 8.1

# Just a minute

GRAMMAR:   Varied
LEVEL:       Elementary to very advanced
TIME:        20 – 30 minutes
MATERIALS:  None

## In class

1  Tell the class you are going to ask one person to speak for sixty seconds without long pauses and without making any grammar mistakes. Stress that in this activity the focus is on grammar, not pronunciation.
   The other members of the group need to listen with their best attention. As soon as someone hears a grammar mistake they challenge the speaker. You need to notice how far through the minute the speaker is when stopped.
   The challenger then tries to correct the mistake. If the correction is right, they get a point (put the student's name and score on the board). The challenger becomes the new speaker and carries on with the same topic for the rest of the minute.
   Should the challenger correct the speaker wrongly, the speaker carries on with the subject to the end of the minute. If the challenger stops the speaker, when the speaker has *not* made a mistake, the speaker carries on and the challenger *loses* a point.
   Sometimes the challenger proposes a wrong correction but someone else shouts out the right correction. In this case, the person who gives the right correction carries on with the subject to the end of the minute and gets the point.
   Whoever is speaking when the minute finishes gets a point.

   **Summary of the rules**
   You *score* a point by:
   – finishing the minute
   – challenging correctly and giving the right correction
   – giving the right correction if the challenger can't
   You *lose* a point by:
   – challenging at a point where nothing is wrong (this means someone may have a negative score)

147

2 Choose the first speaker. Give them a topic, e.g. shoes, boyfriends, cars, dolls, hedgehogs, London etc. Offer them a twenty-second thinking lead-in time and then ask them to start speaking without grammar mistakes. Time the exercise very tightly.

The first time you play the game with a group you may have to encourage the students to challenge. This is especially true with 'polite' groups. Encourage non-verbally – don't succumb to the temptation of challenging yourself. If you do, you kill the game stone dead.

## Variation

Instead of grammar, have the students focus on pronunciation – you have to listen like a dolphin in this version of the game as you will often have to adjudicate on fine points of listening discrimination.

### NOTE

The game is ideal for secondary school classes in places where the students are often bursting with superb energy. It is excellent too with inaccurate, communicative classes at adult level.

The game is *not* right for students who are afraid of speaking because they might make mistakes. The game fails with any group where they decide to take no language risks and only speak at three levels below their real one. The game is group-dynamically interesting in bringing out certain latent or otherwise aggressions. It's an odd game which we have found will work brilliantly with one group and mysteriously not with the next.

### ACKNOWLEDGEMENT

The game presented here is a simplified version of the BBC radio game 'Just a Minute'. In the full version, the players have to speak for a minute without repetition of content words, deviation from the topic or any hesitation or undue pausing. The original version can be played at very advanced levels.

CORRECTION

# 8.2 Correction letters

| | |
|---|---|
| GRAMMAR: | What the student needs to have corrected |
| LEVEL: | Elementary to advanced |
| TIME: | 15 minutes of preparation time per student you choose to use the technique with |
| MATERIAL: | None |

## Preparation

You may have individual students who you feel you can best reach through an exchange of letters. Some students blossom in the written mode. It is perfectly feasible to exchange letters with a few students.*

At the beginning of such correspondences it makes sense to forget about correction. The idea is to get shy students expressing themselves.

Later in a correspondence, and with students you reckon may benefit from direct correction, you can write them 'correction letters'.

What follows is an example of such a letter written in week six of a ten-week intensive course. The student did not get her letter back, so the corrections had to be self standing.

```
Dear Severine,
    How right I am not to have asked you questions. It is
sometimes hard to, but every time I do, I reduce the
freedom you feel to talk of what grabs you.
    If I was to say that all in the Ticino has got an
Italian touch, how would you help me? Let me give you a
clue: a three-letter word has to be replaced by "every-
thing", or at least this is one solution to the problem.
    You know John Wilson keeps telling you English is a
subject—verb—object language? Well, if you look at this
sentence you will see it needs a bit of tinkering with:
'Most people who live in the Italian part of Switzerland
can speak more or less well German.'
    There are lots of things that I used to do as a
child. I used to go ferreting (killed a lot of rabbits),
```

* When I first decided to correspond with some students and not others I was worried about not treating all students equally. It took me a moment to realise that it was fine to use one channel with one student and not with another. Doctors do not prescribe the same medicine for all their patients.

I used to do a lot of cycling and I used to dream of going sailing. I notice you say you used to skiing a lot. You can see my grammar is different from yours.

You must know that after *can* you have the infinitive without *to*, so it is strange to read that it takes you several years until you can skiing. I wonder if you are mixing *can* with *kennen*?

So much for picking up on small glitches in your last letter. I really enjoyed your writing. I get the idea that you are beginning to write English faster than before. Is this the case? You are becoming more sure-footed, like a mountain goat. This is what I seem to see from the outside. Please tell me about the inside. Have you noticed the way Alessandra is really changing the way she is in English for the better?

Tell me a lot more about how a snowboard works etc.

Mario

If you start using the idea of correcting by letter, you will find yourself coming up with many more ways of doing it than those evident in the letter above.

### TEACHING JAPANESE STUDENTS (IF YOU ARE A FOREIGNER TO THEM)

When you first work with a Japanese group you are an outsider. They have to treat you politely, but at arm's length. To get through and to get something of the status of an insider (to go from the *soto* (outside) position to the *uchi* (home) position you might try writing them letters. This is a channel that they really like. They often write better than they speak. In writing they are not hurried – they have ample time to get things right and check the image they are projecting.

### NOTE

For more on letter-writing in EFL, see *Letters*, by Nicky Burbidge et al.

CORRECTION

# 8.3

# Reformulation

GRAMMAR: What comes up – this exercise is most relevant with students who share the same mother tongue
LEVEL: Beginner to advanced
TIME: 10 minutes preparation time
Another 10 minutes preparation time
15 – 30 minutes in fourth class
MATERIALS: (For fourth class) copies of student's original letter and copies of the reformulated letter

## In first class

Ask a student if they would be happy for you to rewrite a piece of their writing and then show both texts to the whole class for correction purposes.

## Preparation

Write the student a letter about whatever interests you and them.

## In second class

Give the student the letter and ask them to bring a reply by the next lesson.

## In third class

Take in the letter. Rewrite it in fully correct and gently enriched English. Try to echo the student's way of writing and don't make the reformulation inaccessibly good.
Photocopy the original letter and your reformulation for the whole class.

## In fourth class

Give out both versions of the student's letter. Ask everybody, working in pairs, to make a list of the mistakes they find when comparing the two versions. The aim of the exercise is to sharpen and feed the students' self-monitoring ability.

## Variation

(for a computer room which is set up as a network)

Ask your students to write letters to each other, using the wordprocessing network. Choose one letter to reformulate on your machine. Twenty-five minutes before the end of the session, send out the reformulated letter for everyone to read. Ask them to erase it from their screens. Now send out the original. Ask everybody to rewrite it from what they remember of your corrections. Finally send out the reformulation again, so they can compare the three texts. (If you don't have your computers set up on a network, but you do have enough freestanding computers, it's relatively easy either to copy enough disks to have one per computer, or to quickly feed in the information to the various computers from one disk.)

## Example

*Original letter from elementary student*

Dear Mario,

thank you for your letter!
Yesterday I have written home at both (my mother and my father), and I have written at any my friends and I have said does hier it's all ok!!
I don't melancholy for my family because hier it's very, very nice! I— When I was in Switzerland I don't see very often my family because they work very hard, my father work in the cook on the evening, and daily he work in the office. I think it's very hard her job!! My mother worked in the restaurant and she is the "Boss" there!
My grandmother and grandfather they come from Salzburg you know?
When I born I was my nationality was Austria, and when I was ten years old, my father naturalised Swiss and I automaticly become swiss.
I think that's very guda have the parents "international" because today I can speak very well Germany!
Germany it's essentiel speak in my country, I am fortunate does I don't have to study this language!

see you,
Michelle

CORRECTION

## Reformulation of Michelle's letter

Dear Mario,

Thank you for your letter. Yesterday I wrote home to both my father and my mother. I have also written to some friends, to tell them everything here is fine.

I don't feel homesick for my family because things are really going swimmingly here. When I was in Switzerland I didn't see my family very often as they work very hard. My father cooks in the evenings and works in his office during the daytime. I think his job is very hard. My mother works in the restaurant and she is the 'boss' there.

My grandparents come from Salzburg. Do you know the place? When I was born I was an Austrian national. When I reached the age of ten my father naturalised Swiss and I automatically became Swiss.

My feeling is that it is good to have 'international' parents because today I can speak really proper German. German is vital in my country. I am lucky not to have to study this language.

See you,

Michelle

REFORMULATION

## 8.4 Mistakes mirror

GRAMMAR: Varied – for students sharing the same mother tongue
LEVEL: Beginner to elementary
TIME: 15 – 20 minutes
MATERIALS: Copies of student's composition (one copy per pair of students)
Copies of mother tongue 'translation' of student's composition (one copy per pair of students)

## Preparation

Choose an average student composition and, after first asking the student's permission, rewrite it in the student's mother tongue, in a way that closely imitates what has gone wrong with the English. So, if the student writes, e.g. 'I am going to lost the bus' and her mother tongue is Spanish, you write '*voy a perdido el bus*'(*voy* = I am going, *a* = to, *perdido* = lost, *el bus* = the bus).

Copy both the mother tongue 'translation' and the original text so you can give one of each to every pair of students.

## In class

1 Give out the mother tongue 'translation' and ask students to work in pairs correcting it.
2 Give out the original and ask them to correct that.

### Variation

This exercise is very similar to a pronunciation one, where you ask students to ham-up an English person speaking their language and then to transfer the most salient sounds to reading a piece of English themselves – within the same mode of dramatic hamming-up.

Both exercises use the mother tongue as a powerful distorting mirror.

### RATIONALE

The point of this exercise is to mirror back to the student in mother tongue the crudity of the mistake they have made in Language 2. The mother tongue is a powerfully understood code and here we are trying to help the student to see Language 2 in the same intense three-dimensional way.

CORRECTION

## 8.5

# Hand on hand

GRAMMAR: Present simple third person singular
LEVEL: Beginner to elementary (or for revision at higher levels)
TIME: 15 minutes
MATERIALS: None

## In class

1 Demonstrate the exercise with one student in front of the group:
   Ask them to think of a person whose daily routine they know really well.
   Do the same yourself. Put your hand on the table and say the first thing
   your person does first thing in the morning, e.g. 'he switches on the
   light'. They put their hand on yours and say what their person does first
   thing, e.g. 'she gets up'. Put your other hand on top of theirs and say the
   second thing your person does.
   Continue this way fast through the day keeping the hand pile going.
2 Pair the students and ask them to do the same exercise.
3 Check on any words they were unsure of.
4 Ask them to pair with new people and do the exercise, thinking of the
   same people's routines, but this time much faster.

RATIONALE

Third person 's' is an insignificant jot of grammar. It's easy to explain,
students understand it, they've been corrected lots of times but they often
forget it. Rather than correct in class, we've found it more efficient to give
them a physically grounded exercise like this one to help them get it right.
If they do subsequently omit third person 's' you can simply touch the back
of their hands with your full palm to remind them – a powerful trigger.
This exercise asks students to do two things at once and so helps them do
the language one a lot better. Parallel processing is mentally helpful. We
need many more exercises that involve such processing.

ACKNOWLEDGEMENT
We learnt this exercise from Grethe Hooper Hanson, President of SEAL
(Society for Effective and Affective Learning), in a workshop at the
Cambridge Academy.

HAND ON HAND

**9.1**

# Listening to time

GRAMMAR: Time phrases
LEVEL: Upper intermediate to very advanced
TIME: 40 – 50 minutes
MATERIALS: None

YOU CAN USE THIS IDEA TO PRACTISE A VARIETY OF DIFFERENT STRUCTURES – SEE VARIATIONS BELOW FOR SOME EXAMPLES

## Preparation

Invite a native speaker to your class, preferably not a language teacher as they sometimes distort their speech. Ask the person to speak about a topic that has them move through time. In one group we asked a South African, from the white minority, to come and talk about his country's history and his recent return there. The talk should last around twenty minutes. Explain to the speaker that the students will be paying close attention not only to the content but to the language form, too.

## In class

1 Before the speaker arrives, explain to the students that they are to jot down all the words and phrases they hear that express time. They don't need to note all the verbs!
2 Welcome the speaker and introduce the topic.
3 The speaker takes the floor for fifteen to twenty minutes and you join the students in taking language notes. If there are questions from the students, make sure that people continue to take language notes during the questioning.
4 Put the students in threes to compare their time-phrase notes. Suggest the speaker joins one of the groups. Some natives are delighted to look in a 'speech mirror'.
5 Share your own notes with the class.
Round off the lesson by picking out other useful and normal bits of language the speaker used that are not yet part of your students' idiolects.

## Example

The South African speaker mentioned above produced these time words: only about ten years / there was a gap of nine years / at roughly the same time / over the next few hundred years / from 1910 until the present day / it's been way back / within eighteen months there will be / until three years ago / when I was back in September

## Variations

Choose a speaker who is about to go off on an important trip. In speaking about this, some of the verbs used will be in a variety of forms used to talk about the future.

Invite someone to speak about the life and habits of someone significant to them, but who lives separately from them, say a grandparent. This topic is likely to evoke a rich mixture of present simple, present continuous, *will* used to describe habitual events, *'ll be -ing* etc.

A past narrative will usually throw up a mixture of past simple, past continuous and past perfect tenses.

### NOTE

To invite the learners to pick specific grammar features out of a stream of live speech is a powerful form of grammar presentation. In this technique the students 'present' the grammar to themselves. They go through a process of realisation which is a lot stronger than what often happens in their minds during the type of 'grammar presentation' required of trainees on many teacher training courses. During a realisation process, they are usually not asleep.

# 9.2 Guess the sentence

GRAMMAR: Varied
LEVEL: Beginner to intermediate
TIME: 20 minutes
MATERIALS: Set of prepared sentences on slips of paper

## Preparation

For each student in your class, prepare a different, thought-provoking sentence that carries the structure you want to present. Write each sentence on a slip of paper.

## In class

1 Make sure all the students have a pencil and rubber.
2 Supposing you are presenting 'adverb order', you might choose a sentence like e.g. 'Poor people always lose their way'. Don't reveal the sentence yet.
   Dictate the first letter: 'capital P'. All the students should write it down.
3 Now invite a student to predict the next letter. Supposing someone says 'A', say 'no' and give them the next letter 'O'.
4 Continue as above. Each time they get a letter wrong, give it to them and ask them to guess the one after. If the letter is right, everyone pencils it in and then has another guess. (Space and full stop count as 'letters'.) With most sentences it's possible to guess a good 50 per cent of the letters in the sentence from context.
5 Give each student a sentence with the structure in it. Tell them not to show their sentences to neighbours. Pair the students. Student A acts as question master for her sentence while student B does the guessing, as outlined in steps 1–4. Student B then acts as question master for her questions.

### Variation

For revision, students can be asked to write their own sentences within the structure, which they then use as in steps 1–4.
This exercise is better demonstrated with a student in front of the class, rather than explained (see notes on giving instructions, page xv).

PRESENTATION

## 9.3 Grammar letters

GRAMMAR: 'Second' conditional
LEVEL: Lower intermediate
TIME: 15 minutes preparation time for the teacher
10 minutes in first class
MATERIALS: A letter to the students, prepared in advance (one copy per student)

THIS ACTIVITY CAN BE ADAPTED FOR USE WITH DIFFERENT STRUCTURES AT ALL LEVELS

## Preparation

Write a letter to all your students introducing the new grammar you have to present. Here is an example of one I wrote to a lower intermediate class:

```
Dear Everybody,
    Do you ever dream about what it would be like if you were
quite different from the way you are? I sometimes do. Let me
share a dream with you.
    Suppose I was a woman, I'd be a bit scared to walk around
Canterbury at night.
    If I were a woman, I don't think I'd ever buy nylon
tights because they only last a few days.
    If I was a woman, I'd feel quite differently about the
students in this class. I'd probably feel closer to Michelle,
but I might find Dorota more difficult.
    Had I been born a woman, what kind of husband would I
have married?
    If I were my children's mother … No, I just can't imagine
what it would be like.
    My feeling is that if I were a woman I'd be a lot freer
in society than I am as a man. I realise that some of you
will disagree with this.
    Please notice the grammar around 'if'. Read the sentences
above again, thinking about their grammar.
    For your next homework imagine yourself changing sex.
Please write me a letter about the consequences for you of
changing sex.
```

Maybe you don't want to think in this area. If you don't
want to write about this, then imagine that you wake up one
morning Japanese (if you are Japanese then imagine you wake
up one morning as a really surprising gai-jin!). Or imagine
that Switzerland has suddenly become an island in the middle
of the Atlantic. Maybe it really is! Think of the Canaries
where Switzerland is now.
    I'm looking forward to a long letter from each of you.

    Mario

# In class

1 Give each student a copy of your letter and allow time for them to read the text. Help with vocabulary or grammar problems. This may involve you in reinforcing the written grammar presentation in the letter. Tell the students that your letter gives them all the grammar they need in order to reply.

2 Collect in the letters in the next class. Don't waste time marking them. Pick out a few of the most interesting ones in terms of human content and grammar misunderstanding. Photocopy these for the whole group.

3 Give the class copies of the letters you have chosen to highlight. Let them read them, enjoying them for content. Then go through the main grammar difficulties.

RATIONALE

Why is grammar in language classes nearly always presented orally and sometimes at pretty high speed compared to the gentle, individual pace of reading? Do all learners take it in better this way? Here are some advantages to presenting grammar via a letter:

- The new patterns become part of a personal communication from you to the class – you are teaching them the structures via your thoughts and feelings. My students found out one or two new things about me as a person, when they read the conditional letter above. The grammar is coming across in teacher, first-person voice, not in third-person 'textbookese'.

- You can adjust the level of difficulty in your presentation of the grammar to the various levels you know to be present in your group, in a way that the poor coursebook writer could never have foreseen.

- The most successful language learners catch it from their mothers – in this situation language is highly infectious. Your students are more likely to be infected with the foreign language from your person than from the pages of any book.

– Letter presentation of grammar allows quiet students to work at their own pace. It allows students to practise the structures in writing before they have to blurt them out orally. This suits some better.

When you have tried this exercise with your students you will probably be able to add a few more to this list of advantages.

### NOTE ON LETTER-WRITING CULTURE

Quite a lot of teachers have discovered how powerful letter-writing can be as a classroom tool. Our colleague Félix Salmones de García in Santander, Spain, has his secondary school children write letters to children all over the world. He prefers them writing to non-native speaking children, as this then allows him to do indirect grammar correction. Félix picks a letter sent by a boy in Cairo, say, and focuses with his class on those mistakes the Spanish children make as well. He finds this indirect correction seems to feel much less ego-corrosive to the student than frontal correction of their own work.

Mike Gradwell, working at ESIEE, a Grande École near Paris, regularly has his electronics engineers write letters across the classroom. Some of these letters are too private in their nature to allow him to do correction work on. About 50 per cent can be put into a correction pool and get worked on for language.

Félix and Mike are just two examples of teachers who have created a kind of letter-writing state of mind in their groups, a letter-writing culture. If this area interests you, have a look at *Letters*, by Nicky Burbidge et al.

# 9.4

# 'The' and 'a'

GRAMMAR: Articles / *another* / *the other* / *the last* / *one* / *ones*
LEVEL: Beginner (or at higher levels as a review)
TIME: 25 minutes
MATERIALS: Lots of pens of three or four different colours

## Preparation

You'll need about twenty brightly coloured pens. Ideally there should be four or five in three different colours and some twos or singles in other colours.

## In class

1 Ask one of the students to come up and sit near you at an empty table. Make sure all the rest of the class has a good view of the table.
2 Hold all the pens upright in a bunch in the centre of the table. Release them, letting them fall at random.
3 Give the student at your side instructions as follows: 'Take a blue one. Take the blue one on the right. Take another blue one. Take the last blue one. Take a red one. Take another red one. Take the rest of the red ones. Take the brown one. Take the green one on the left. Take a green one.' etc.
   Carry on until the table has been cleared by the student. If at any time the student can't follow your instructions, repeat two or three times until they get it. If the student misunderstands, indicate that they should replace the pen and you repeat the instruction.
4 Repeat step 3 if you think the students need another model. Otherwise reverse the process and get the student to instruct you. You simply obey the student's instructions when their utterance is correct. Do and say nothing when they're not correct (the fact that you haven't taken a pen is a clear indication that they have made a mistake). Continue until the table is clear.
5 Repeat the exercise until you are sure most of the students have got the grammar. Organise small groups of students. Get them to empty and pool their pencil cases and try the exercise in small groups.

PRESENTATION

## NOTE 1

To make the exercise a little more difficult, in step 5 change the rules so that the students must instruct the others to pick at least two pens of different colours at a time, e.g. 'Take a blue one and the last two red ones.'

## NOTE 2

It's worth having a quick practice in the staffroom with a colleague to make sure you keep your language natural in the class.
Cuisinaire rods are good for this exercise. So are sweets or biscuits of different types.

# Word order dictation

| | |
|---|---|
| GRAMMAR: | Word order at sentence level |
| | The grammar you decide to input – in this example: reflexive phrases, e.g. *to myself / by myself / in myself* |
| LEVEL: | Intermediate |
| TIME: | 20 – 30 minutes |
| MATERIALS: | **Jumbled extracts** (for dictation) |
| | One copy of **Extract from Sarah's letter** per pair of students |

## In class

1 Pair the students and ask one person in each pair to prepare to write on a loose sheet of paper.
2 Dictate the first sentence from the **Jumbled extracts**. One person in each pair takes it down.
3 Ask the pairs to rewrite the jumbled words into a meaningful sentence, using all the words and putting in necessary punctuation.
4 Tell the pairs to pass their papers to the right. The pairs receiving their neighbours' sentences check out grammar and spelling, correcting where necessary.
5 Dictate the second jumbled sentence.
6 Repeat steps 3 and 4.
7 When you've dictated all the sentences in this way give out the original, unjumbled **Extract from Sarah's letter** and ask the students to compare with the sentences they've got in front of them. They may sometimes have created excellent, viable alternative sentences.

### JUMBLED EXTRACTS

1 myself in absorbed more and more becoming am I find I
2 when mix I do other with people me inside a confusion have I I find
3 David John and Nick as though I am me I do not feel when I walk through the park with
4 strange seems it and a role acting am I like feel I
5 walk park myself talk aloud myself to I by the through I when
6 completely feel content I

## Variation

You can happily use a coursebook presentational text in the way outlined above. It may enhance its interest.

ACKNOWLEDGEMENT

The **Extract from Sarah's letter** comes from *Sarah's Letters – a Case of Shyness* by Bernard T. Harrison. Olinka Breka taught us this technique, which she told us was partly based on the 'Pass the buck' exercise in *Dictation* that we wrote in the 1980's. And so methodology develops, as exercises jump from mind to mind, weaving off the printed page and back into the oral transmission that goes on between teachers. Who will hear this exercise from you and marvellously add to it?

# 9.6  Guess my grammar

GRAMMAR: Varied + question forms
LEVEL: Elementary to intermediate
TIME: 55 minutes
MATERIALS: None

## In class

1 Choose a grammar area the students need to review. In the example below there are adjectives, adverbs and relative pronouns.

2 Ask each student to work alone and write a sentence of 12 – 16 words (the exact length is not too important). Each sentence should contain an adjective, and adverb and a relative pronoun, or whatever grammar you've chosen to practise. For example: 'She sat quietly by the golden river that stretched to the sea.'

3 Now ask the students to rewrite their sentences on a separate piece of paper, leaving in the target grammar and any punctuation, but leaving the rest as blanks, one dash for each letter. The sentence above would look like this:

––– ––– quietly –– ––– golden ––––– that ––––––––– –– ––– –––

While they're doing this ask any students who are not sure of the correctness of their sentence to check with you.

4 Now ask the students to draw a picture or pictures which illustrate as much of the meaning of the sentence as possible. For example, for the sentence above they might draw:

PRESENTATION

5 As students finish drawing, put them into groups of three. One person shows the blanked sentence and the drawing, reserving their original sentence for their own reference. The other two should guess: 'Is the first word *the*?' or ask questions 'Is the second word a verb?' etc. The student should only answer 'yes' or 'no'. As they guess the words, they fill in the blanks.

6 They continue until all the blanks are filled and then they do the other two persons' sentences.

### NOTE

Groups tend to finish this activity at widely different speeds. If a couple of groups finish early, pair them across the groups, ask them to rub out the completed blanked out sentences and try them on a new partner.

### ACKNOWLEDGEMENT

Ian Jasper originated this exercise. He is a co-author of *Teacher Development: One Group's Experience*, edited by Janie Rees Miller.

## 9.7    Teacherless task

| | |
|---|---|
| GRAMMAR: | Past simple and past perfect |
| LEVEL: | First example **Strip story A**: upper intermediate to advanced |
| | Second example **Strip story B**: intermediate |
| TIME: | 15 – 30 minutes |
| MATERIALS: | One cut-up **Strip story** per ten students |
| | One copy of complete **Strip story** per student |

### Preparation

Copy the **Strip story** below. If you have thirty students, make three copies and cut these up into strips, keeping the sets of strips separate. You need one set of strips per ten students. You also need a copy of the whole **Strip story** per student, for the end of the lesson.

### In class

1  Seat the students in circles of as near to ten as possible.
2  Give out a copy of the story, cut into strips, to each group. (Make sure the strips are out of sequence.) Within the group, each student takes one strip. Ask the students to read their mini-texts silently and to ask your help with words they don't know.
3  Explain that the aim of the game is to sequence the strips into a story and to solve the problem it poses.
   **Rule 1:**   Only read your own strip of paper. You are not allowed to look at anyone else's.
   **Rule 2:**   Don't write.
   **Rule 3:**   Only ask the teacher language questions.
   With some groups it is enough to give them the aim of the game and the rules – with others, you need to tell them to proceed by reading their strips aloud round the group. Beyond this, leave the methodology they use for tackling the task entirely up to them, within the rules, of course. Don't intervene and make suggestions – you are likely to mess up the dynamics of the circles if you do.
4  The circles of ten students sequence the story and solve the problem. This is a time for you to listen diagnostically to pronunciation mistakes and to watch the dynamics of each group.

5 Once the students have found the solution, give each person a copy of the full text.

---

**STRIP STORY A**

*The unopened letter*

There once was a country where people believed that the longer you leave a letter unopened, the worse the contents get. So, a letter of complaint delayed in the post or left unopened would become a hate letter. Bills would get more expensive the longer they were unopened.

Maria was sitting in a café when she saw her husband, who she'd just got divorced from, sitting with his new wife, Sophia. They looked so happy together.

She went home and wrote this letter:
Dear Gregory,
I now know that you love her and don't love me. This is the last time you will ever hear from me.
Maria

Because Maria had got the postcode wrong, it was not until some days later that Sophia found the letter on her doormat. Gregory was away that week on business. She phoned him. He told her not to worry but to bring the letter on Friday, when she was going to visit him in the place he was working.

Friday night in the new city: they had a wonderful dinner and went back to their hotel. Just as they were going to bed, Sophia remembered to remind him about the letter in her bag. But he felt it would spoil the evening and felt peeved.

He lay in bed, unable to sleep. He wanted to get the letter, but every time he moved his wife stirred in her sleep and he was afraid of waking her.

---

All day Saturday they thought about the letter but neither of them got round to suggesting they open it. When they had finished lunch on Sunday, and just as she was about to catch her train back, something came over Sophia. She took the letter out of her bag and flung it across the table, before running out into the rain.

Grabbing his umbrella and the letter, he caught up with her in the square. Her hair in the rain looked so beautiful. He thought how Maria, his first wife, would never have come out without an umbrella. Sophia soon calmed down, but noticed he had taken time to carefully bring his umbrella. He immediately gave it to the nearest person without one.

After he had seen her off on her train, he walked slowly through the streets, stopping a couple of times to have a drink. Back at the hotel he opened the letter.

The letter bore out the belief of the people in that country: letters get worse if you leave them unopened. How had the letter got worse? This is the problem you have to solve.

*Solution to* **Strip story A**

Dear Gregory,
I now know you love her and don't love me. This is the last time you will ever hear from me.
Sophia

PRESENTATION

## Telling the time

Jane went into a restaurant and ordered some soup.

When she had finished she asked for the bill, which came to eight francs.

She began counting out the money 'One, two, three...' and then said, 'Oh, what time is it?'

The waitress looked at her watch, 'Five, Madam' and Jane went on counting out the francs, 'six, seven, eight'.

An old man sitting in the corner had been watching this going on. He thought he'd do the same.

He came back next day at lunchtime and ordered some soup.

When he'd finished he called for the bill which came to eight francs.

He started counting out the money 'One, two, three ...' and then said, 'Oh, what time is it?'

The waitress looked at her watch 'One, Sir' and the old man went on counting, '... two, three, four, five, six, seven, eight'.

How much money had the waitress lost on these two transactions?

© Cambridge University Press 1995

TEACHERLESS TASK

> *Solution to Strip story B*
>
> The waitress lost two francs and then made two francs. Overall she lost nothing.
>
> © Cambridge University Press 1995

## Variation

The 'teacherless task' idea originates in management training. You can use it the way it is used there: pull out some observers (say two per circle of ten) and ask them to take detailed notes on how the leadership roles pass round the circles (or don't). Once the task has been accomplished, ask the observers to feed back what they have noticed to their circle, or to the whole group.

### RATIONALE

As the students sequence the story, they will be soaking up the grammar we have built in. If you work in the 'Presentation, Controlled practice, Free practice' frame, then 'teacherless tasks' are ideal for an amalgamation of the first two phases.

### NOTE

If 'teacherless tasks' appeal to your classes you will find twenty of them in *Towards the Creative Teaching of English* by Spaventa, Langenheim, Melville and Rinvolucri, Pilgrims and Heinemann, 1980. **Strip story B** 'Telling the time' is reprinted from this book, which has been out of print since 1992.

The stories above are presented broken up into ten parts. If you have odd numbered groups it's quite easy to rewrite the story for different numbers.

PRESENTATION

## 9.8

# Puzzle stories

GRAMMAR: Simple present and simple past interrogative forms
LEVEL: Beginners
TIME: 30 minutes
MATERIALS: **Puzzle story** (to be written on the board)

## Preparation

Ask a couple of students from an advanced class to come to your beginners group. Explain that they will have some interesting interpreting to do. (Should your class be multilingual see note below.)

## In class

1 Introduce the interpreters to your class and welcome them.
2 Write this **Puzzle story** on the board in English. Leave good spaces between the lines:

There were three people in the room.
A man spoke.
There was a short pause.
The second man spoke.
The woman jumped up and slapped the first man in the face.

Ask one of the beginners to come to the board and underline the words they know. Ask others to come and underline the ones they know. Tell the group the words none of them know. Ask one of the interpreters to write a translation into mother tongue. The translation should come under the respective line of English.

3 Tell the students their task is to find out why the woman slapped the first man. They are to ask questions that you can answer 'yes' or 'no'. Tell them they can try and make questions directly in English, or they can call the interpreter and ask the question in their mother tongue. The interpreter will whisper the English in their ear and they then ask you in English.

4 Erase the mother tongue translation of the story from the board.

5 One of the interpreters moves round the room interpreting questions while the other stays at the board and writes up the questions in both English and mother tongue.

6 You should aim to let the class ask about 15–25 questions, more will overload them linguistically. To speed the process up you should give them clues.

7 Finally, have the students copy the questions written on the board into their books. You now have a presentation of the main interrogative forms of the simple present and past. How will you work on from this student-produced language data?

8 After the lesson go through any problems the interpreters had – offer them plenty of parallel translations.

The solution

The second man was an interpreter.


## Further material

Do you know the one about the seven-year-old who went to the baker's? His Mum had told him to get three loaves. He went in, bought two and ran home. He put them on the kitchen table. He ran back to the baker's and bought a third. He rushed in and put the third one on the kitchen table. Solution: He had a speech defect and couldn't say 'Th'. You'll find another twenty such stories in *Challenge to Think*, by Marge Berer, Christine Frank and Mario Rinvolucri. You'll need the Teacher's Book if you want the solutions!

You will find another, fiercer, use of puzzle stores in *Grammar Games*, p. 84, 'With your back to the class'.

### NOTE

This exercise can also be done in multilingual classes. You need a translator for each mother tongue represented in the group, and a large blackboard for all the translations. (An alternative could be for the translators to give their translations orally, or on slips of paper to their sub-groups.)

### ACKNOWLEDGEMENT

We wouldn't have come up with this exercise without the pioneering work of Charles Curran and Earl Stevick, who both believe that beginners in a second language can and should originate the text through which they learn the language. Charles Curran has left us 'Community Language Learning' (see p. 106–11 of *Dictation*, by Paul Davis and Mario Rinvolucri) and Stevick's 'Islamabad' game is a classic of language teaching (see *A Way and Ways* by Earl Stevick and (2.12) p. 56–57 of this book).

PRESENTATION

# Bibliography

Baudains, Richard and Baudains, Marjorie. *Alternatives*, Longman, 1990.

Berer, Marge and Frank, Christine and Rinvolucri, Mario. *Challenge to Think*, Oxford University Press, 1982.

Bowen, Tim and Marks, Jonathan. *The Pronunciation Book*, Pilgrims / Longman, 1992.

Bowers, Roger et al. *Talking about Grammar*, Longman, 1987.

Burbidge, Nicky et al. *Letters*, Oxford University Press, forthcoming 1996.

Davis, Paul and Rinvolucri, Mario. *The Confidence Book*, Pilgrims / Longman, 1990.

Davis, Paul and Rinvolucri, Mario. *Dictation*, Cambridge University Press, 1988.

Deller, Sheelagh. *Lessons from the Learners*. Pilgrims / Longman, 1990.

Frank, Christine and Rinvolucri, Mario. *Grammar in Action Again*, Pilgrims / Prentice-Hall International, 1987.

Lindstromberg, Seth (editor). *The Recipe Book*, Pilgrims / Longman, 1990.

Morgan, John and Rinvolucri, Mario. *Once Upon a Time*, Cambridge University Press, 1983.

Moskowitz, Gertrude. *Caring and Sharing in the Foreign Language Classroom*, Newbury House, 1972.

Rees Miller, Janie (editor). *Teacher Development – One Group's Experience*, unpublished manuscript.

Rinvolucri, Mario. *Grammar Games*, Cambridge University Press, 1984.

Sinclair, John (editor). *Collins COBUILD English Grammar*, Collins, 1990.

Sinclair, John (editor). *Collins COBUILD English Usage*, HarperCollins, 1992.

Spaventa, Lou (editor) et al. *Towards the Creative Teaching of English*, Heinemann, 1980.

Stevick, Earl. *A Way and Ways*, Newbury House, 1980.

*Games, Games, Games*. (a Woodcraft Folk handbook sold in Oxfam shops in UK)

# Acknowledgements

We would like to thank several groups of Cambridge Academy students for their part in being the first end-users of this book. They taught us a lot.
We would also like to thank our patient editors, Jeanne McCarten and Nóirín Burke, for much improving the book.
There is a special thrill for authors when they work through the suggestions, criticisms and hurrays of teachers who have read and piloted the original manuscript. So a big hug to our readers and piloters.

*Paul and Mario*

The authors and publishers are grateful to the following individuals and institutions who have given permission to reproduce copyright material. It has not been possible to identify the sources of all the material used and in such cases the publishers would welcome information from copyright owners.

© *The Guardian* 1992 for the extract (p. 38); Japan National Tourist Organization for the photograph (p. 38); *The Independent* for the extract *Sensible advice* by Simon Carr (p. 70); The Institute of Education, University of London for the extract from *Sarah's letters* by Bernard T. Harrison, Bedford Way Papers, 1986 (p. 164); John Williams for the photograph of Mario Rinvolucri (inside back cover); Stuart Oglethorpe for the photograph of Paul Davis (inside back cover).

Design by Newton Harris
Illustrations by Nicky Dupays, Annie Farrall and Pete Neame
Cover illustration by Nicky Dupays